Hamsters

in Your Life

Critter Press

Critter Press
A Simon & Schuster Macmillan Company
1633 Broadway
New York, NY 10019

ISBN 0-87605-438-6

Cataloging-in-Publication data available upon request from the
Library of Congress

Manufactured in the United States of America

10 9 8 7 6 5 4 3 2 1

SERIES DIRECTOR: AMANDA PISANI
ASSISTANT DIRECTOR: JENNIFER LIBERTS
ILLUSTRATION BY BRYAN TOWSE
BOOK DESIGN BY MICHELE LASEAU
COVER DESIGN BY AMY TROMBAT
PRODUCTION BY TRUDY COLER, STEPHANIE HAMMETT, CLINT LAHNEN,
DENNIS SHEEHAN, TERRI SHEEHAN, CHRIS VAN CAMP

Photography: Front cover photos by Reneé Stockdale
Joan Balzarini: 2–3, 16, 52, 64, 67, 68, 76, 79, 82, 85
Trenna Gordon: 34
Cheryl Primeau: 5, 13, 14, 24, 50, 77, 89
Betsy Sikora Siino: 25, 26
Reneé Stockdale: 7, 8, 9, 11, 12, 15(top), 19, 20, 21, 22–23, 27, 29, 30, 31, 33, 35, 36, 37, 38, 40, 42, 43, 45, 46, 48, 51, 54, 55, 56, 58, 65, 66, 69, 72–73, 74, 75, 78, 81, 84, 86, 87, 88, 91, 92
B. Everett Webb: 15(bottom)

Contents

part one
Welcome to the World of the

Hamster

External Features of the Hamster

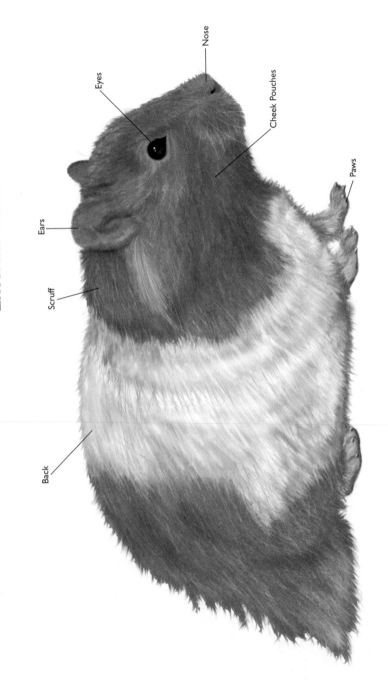

Eyes

Nose

Cheek Pouches

Paws

Ears

Scruff

Back

Hamsters as

Pets

A Revolutionary Discovery

The hamster has come a long way from her existence as a golden shorthaired rodent in the wild to a popular pet that may sport any variation of coat type or color and reside in domestic homes—many of those with children.

The hamster's story as a household pet began with a false and relatively late start when she was discovered for the first time in the early 1830s. She went on to enjoy a brief period of popularity as a pet, primarily in England. But despite their prolific breeding habits, the novelty of owning these small, unique, tailless rodents wore off and so did the existence of hamsters in captivity.

Rodents and Humans

Imagine a vast forest, home for centuries to a complex, inter-connected ecosystem of thousands of birds, mammals, insects and plants. Now imagine that forest is razed for cattle grazing or stripped for building identical tract homes. Just where do those resident animals go?

From Dry Beginnings

Did you know that your fuzzy pet—queen of her Habitrail—once roamed the desert? The hamster has evolved from survival in a hostile desert environment, known for extreme temperatures, a lack of shelter and a periodic scarcity of food.

Those species that cannot adapt to human encroachment into their habitats are doomed either to displacement because of the loss of their food supplies and living space, or to outright destruction. This latter fate has typically resulted from intentionally destructive acts on the part of humans. Most predator species, for example, have been targeted for destruction by interloping humans, predators themselves, who have historically viewed their nonhuman counterparts on the food chain as competition.

To their credit, rodents for the most part, even those targeted just as vigorously for destruction, have not suffered the same sad fate as the predators. In fact, they have generally emerged survivors of human activity.

The names of only a few of the planet's hundreds of rodent species appear on the various lists that track the threatened and endangered species of the world. In light of the condition of most animal populations today, that is truly amazing. While individuals who do not care to coexist with mice, rats and their brethren may not be impressed by this fact, even they must admire how nature has enabled these rodent survivors to persist so efficiently.

Survival Techniques

Because most are of relatively small size, rodents may often reside somewhat unobtrusively in the midst of human domiciles, often living right under human noses for weeks or even months before a telltale chewed corner of a sack of flour or birdseed alerts their two-legged hosts to their presence.

Diet has also played a key role in rodent survival. Their physiological makeup enables most rodents to thrive on a variety of foodstuffs, thus ensuring that even when their favored or traditional dietary items disappear, there are always alternatives available. Most rodents can survive on a veritable smorgasbord of options, including vegetarian fare or foods of animal origin including insects and worms.

In terms of physical similarities, most rodent species are relatively small and compact. They use their delicate little "hands" to carry out a variety of functions, including collecting and manipulating food and grooming. Some rodents, such as the hamster, are graced with ample cheek pouches, in which they can store large amounts of food to hide away for a time when food is not so plentiful—a rainy day, if you will.

Clean, quiet, cute, odorless: What more could a pet owner ask for?

The Road to Domesticity

Once in the care of humans, hamsters were first enlisted as laboratory animals, an unpleasant fate to be sure, but one that led to an increase in the understanding of keeping the animals healthy in captivity. This information would later prove vital to the success of keeping hamsters as pets.

Today, hamsters continue to be used as lab animals, although the numbers of hamsters used for this purpose have declined substantially in the last twenty years or so.

Eventually, the hamster's reputation as a quiet, gentle animal (attributes that made it a desirable laboratory animal in the first place) spread. Hardly a surprise to those who had come to know her, the hamster soon found herself being targeted for a far more positive fate—that of a family pet.

Hamster Character

As with all animals that have come to occupy a domestic niche, the hamster's physical and behavioral characteristics have been molded through the ages by her native home, the desert. Understand the link between the hamster's home territory and the appearance, behavior and character of the contemporary pet hamster within your home, and you will be better equipped to enjoy your pet. You will also be better prepared to offer her the optimum care required to keep a hamster spry and healthy until the ripe old age of two or three.

Hamsters make a fascinating first pet for children.

Native Territory

In the golden hamster's ancient homeland, the daytime temperatures were generally warm, the night temperatures cool; food was intermittently scarce and abundant; and there was little vegetation and land-scaping to safely conceal a tiny rodent from predators. Now envision a quiet, gentle animal—the hamster—in the midst of such a scene and evaluate how the characteristics of her native territory relate to the hamster's evolution.

From a physical perspective, this is a small rodent whose large expressive eyes offer the first clue to how this animal would operate in the wild. A nocturnal creature requires large eyes to see effectively in the darkness. In the wild, she spends most of her waking hours under the cover of night, waiting until the atmosphere cools to seek her dinner. The hamster's prominent ears also have a story to tell. They are positioned high on the animal's head so the hamster might best take advantage of her acute sense of hearing, especially when faced with the challenge of detecting the presence of an approaching predator—or the voice of a trusted owner.

The ample cheek pouches are another survival function of the hamster. The hamster can stuff her pouches with almost half her body weight in food, which may then be hidden in private caches for another day when food is not so plentiful (a habit pet hamsters may practice in captivity as well). This would certainly explain why this animal's name is derived from the German word *hamstern,* meaning "to hoard."

This hamster with stuffed cheeks is enjoying a nap after her meal.

As far as hamster behavior is concerned, not much is known about the hamster's life in the wild, and apparently that is precisely how the hamster has intended it to be. The golden hamster remained unknown to the public at large for so long (and her natural wild existence still remains somewhat of an enigma) because of her rather mysterious lifestyle.

Natural Burrowers

This is a lifestyle that took place primarily underground. A consummate burrower, the wild hamster spent a great deal of her time beneath the surface of the earth, hiding in the cool catacombs of tunnels, safe from the harsh rays of the sun, the extreme temperatures and the teeth and claws of rodent-hungry predators. She would emerge from her safe, cool sanctuary when the sun set to scavenge for her dinner.

Food was scarce in the hamster's native territory, a condition that subsequently served to mold the hamster into an animal that requires a great deal of exercise. In the wild, she was forced to travel vast distances to find sustenance. Joke as we might about hamsters running aimlessly on their exercise wheels—miles and miles in a single day—the hamster is driven by instinct to a life of activity.

Hamster owners need to understand that their pets will live longer and more contentedly if they are provided with appropriate and variegated opportunities to play and interact with people. This means making far more of an effort than simply supplying the animal with 24-hour access to an exercise wheel, to which the hamster can become addicted, not to mention exhausted and dehydrated.

A Solitary Pet

The conditions of the hamster's native land, a barren landscape combined with a scarcity of food, were not conducive to sustaining large colonies of hamsters. The animals thus evolved into solitary creatures that fended for themselves. They typically came together only to mate, the female then taking on the responsibility of raising her young on her own. Assuming incorrectly that a single hamster is a lonely hamster, many owners ignore the natural solitary nature of these animals and insist on housing them together, usually with dire, and quite violent, results.

Hamster personality is also often misunderstood. Although hamsters usually prefer the company of humans to that of their own kind, they are frequently labeled mean and ornery. In most instances, the hamster that lives up to those labels is simply a hamster that has been mistreated or was never socialized to human

Why a Hamster?

In a survey conducted by the American Pet Products Manufacturers Association, the hamster has consistently been voted the most popular small pet of the 1990s. Most people who have cast their votes for the hamster feel that they are fun to watch and that they are good educational pets for children.

handling. The well-bred, well-socialized hamster that is properly housed, entertained and cared for should be a gentle, sweet-natured animal that comes to know and trust her owner and to enjoy the time they spend together. Indeed the bond that can form between a hamster and a human can be surprisingly sound and touching.

The hamster, though the ideal pocket pet for the right owner, must not simply be locked in a cage and ignored. She is a solitary creature, but thrives on human care to help her adjust to life in captivity. Cleanliness, play, a healthy diet, a stress-free environment and regular human interaction are the ingredients vital to the health and well-being of this animal that boasts a long and prestigious record of survival.

Look at your hamster in light of her existence as a wild creature and you will find the best of both worlds living within your home: a delightful, gentle, entertaining pet and a creature of the wilderness all wrapped up in a single, rather adorable, package. What an honor to share your home with so distinctive a character.

This sweet-natured hamster is a direct result of an owner who spends time socializing and caring for her pet.

Choosing and Preparing for Your Hamster

Who doesn't love a hamster? Even if someone isn't crazy about rodents because of an experience with mice or rats that invaded the kitchen, most people can't help but notice the sweet, big-eyed mug of the hamster and smile.

The hamster's charm creeps up subtly. You admire his compact, barrel-like physique, his wide muzzle accentuated by a treat hidden within the cheeks and his bright eyes and rather large nose. These characteristics comprise a portrait of a pet that resembles a tiny stuffed toy or living miniature teddy bear. Heeding your first impression, you regard the hamster as a quiet, benign, unobtrusive little creature, until suddenly you recognize something so lovable about this little rodent that you simply must spend the rest of your life basking in that charm.

Wanted: Responsible Owner

Fine examples of happy, healthy hamsters are invariably rooted with the responsible owner. This is a person who takes the time—before bringing a new pet home—to learn about the housing, diet, exercise and social interaction the pet will require if he is to live a long and healthy life.

Whether one is keeping a dog or a tiny dwarf hamster as a pet, an animal deserves optimum living conditions, regular attention as well as veterinary care.

The hamster owner should know the basics of hamster care and be willing to make the time and effort to do it right. The owner needs to understand the hamster's need for cleanliness and make the effort to keep his habitat sanitary. The hamster's bedding should be changed regularly, his food fresh and well-balanced and his access to clean, clear water constant. His owner should respect the hamster's nocturnal habits and reserve playtimes for hours of the day—afternoon and evening—when he is most amenable to activity.

With adult supervision, kids can provide a responsible and loving home for a hamster.

A responsible owner can be an adult or a child (many a child has actually proven to be the superior caretaker in this endeavor). A hamster is a fine pet choice for children, although his care must never be relegated exclusively to a child. While caring for a hamster presents a child with the opportunity to learn the importance of providing a pet with food, water, attention and a clean environment, this must be done with adult supervision should the child lose interest or inclination.

The greatest part of being a responsible owner is the commitment made to the hamster. The individual should be dedicated to providing the hamster with all the necessary amenities, avoiding unintentional breeding and spending time every day with his or her pet. In return, the owner will learn how attached people can become to these wee creatures, and what a delightful relationship can exist between what was once a solitary desert dweller and the lucky person who takes him in. This often comes as a surprise to first-time owners who find themselves hooked for life after that first experience of living in harmony with a hamster.

It's important to be committed to making your hamster feel like part of the family.

Where to Purchase Your New Pet

Once you have decided that the hamster is the pet for you (and determined whether you would like a golden hamster with long or short hair, or perhaps a dwarf) you should begin the search for your companion. Several options are available.

The Pet Store

The most popular place for obtaining a hamster is the pet store. While many pet shops these days are opting not to sell puppies and kittens, most still carry small pocket pets, a group to which the hamster belongs.

The benefit of the pet shop is the convenience it presents. Find a good shop with a knowledgeable staff, and you can take advantage of one-stop shopping. This enables you to buy the hamster and necessary supplies for his care at the same location.

Look for a shop with a well-educated staff that can answer questions about the care of the pets they are placing. They should offer sound advice on hamster care and be able to tell the difference between male hamsters and females (a male's testicles are usually quite recognizable). The shop should be sanitary—evident in the animals' clean food and water and general lack of odor. The pets within the shop should look healthy and well adjusted, their habitats clean and uncrowded.

Hamsters in the pet shop should, in most cases, be housed separately. The exceptions may be younger siblings, which may be housed together, and dwarf hamsters which are more social in nature than are their golden cousins and thus more amenable to cohabitation. The ideal, however, is separate housing, which indicates that the store understands the solitary nature of hamsters, and also reduces the risk that you'll discover an unexpected hamster pregnancy once you get your new pet home.

Hamsters should generally be kept separately, in clean and spacious habitats.

These young siblings are being housed together.

The Breeder

If you want a more exotic hamster—say, a teddy bear (long-haired) hamster of a specific color or pattern—then the breeder is usually your best bet. Hamster breeders may be difficult to locate in a given area, so you may have to do some hunting.

In your search for a hamster breeder, check the newspaper. Some advertise, and you may be able to find them easily.

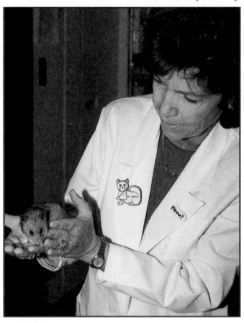

You may also want to ask the local pet shops that carry hamsters, as the breeders from whom they obtain their animals may breed exotic varieties. Ask local veterinarians, as well, especially those that treat hamsters. They should know breeders in the area who are their clients (this also shows that the breeder is willing to work with a veterinarian).

Another locale for finding breeders—especially several breeders all congregated together—is at

A veterinarian is a good resource for finding a reputable hamster breeder.

a county or state fair. Hamsters are among the displays of the many animals that you will find at fairs. The individuals handling those hamsters are usually their breeders, most of whom couldn't be happier to speak with prospective buyers who appreciate the quality of fine show hamsters.

The Animal Shelter

As part of that endless cycle of too many hamsters and not enough homes, some of those abandoned or homeless hamsters find themselves at the doorstep of the local animal shelter. What happens to them at that point depends on the shelter and the resources available to it.

Some shelters have set up hamster adoption programs and encourage would-be hamster owners to visit the many fine animals available for adoption. But others, because they are overwhelmed with the vast numbers of dogs and cats that come their way, have no choice but to humanely euthanize the small rodents. Unfortunately they simply do not have the staff, money or space to accommodate the hamsters. Contact your local shelters as possible sources for a hamster—and consider the overcrowded pet population when thinking of breeding your pet.

Choosing a Healthy Hamster

Regardless of where you obtain your hamster, the criteria by which you choose your new pet should be taken seriously. Whether purchasing a hamster from a pet store, from a breeder at a county fair or from an animal shelter, consider the following points when evaluating potential pets.

Age

No matter how you slice it, hamsters do not have long life spans. Most live for two to three years.

Most people naturally prefer a younger hamster, as the young pets' minimal experience with humans allows the new owner to easily socialize him. This does not mean an older hamster is out of the question, however. An older hamster, with gentle handling, can bond to new people as well, especially if his experience with humans has been positive.

As for the older hamster, who may have had negative experiences with humans, you can enjoy a mutually satisfying relationship with this animal, but on his terms. He may never enjoy the handling that some pets delight in, yet he can still partake in daily forays out of his enclosure and take comfort in the fact that he is cared for each day by an owner who does not force him into uncomfortable situations. You, in turn, may take pride in knowing that with this compassion you are rekindling a hamster's faith in humans.

> **Signs of a Healthy Hamster**
>
> Bright, lively eyes
>
> Clean, erect ears
>
> Well-formed and trimmed incisors
>
> Hearty appetite
>
> Barrel-shaped physique
>
> Alert expression

Male or Female?

While hamsters exhibit differences in behavior during mating, most veteran hamster owners do not see a dramatic difference between the two as pets. This is probably because they are solitary animals and housed individually.

While you may not have a preference from a hamster keeping perspective, gender can play an important role in unexpected pregnancies. You are best off working with breeders, pet shop staff and shelter personnel who are well-versed in telling males from females (which can be difficult among young hamsters). To be safe, always follow the separate housing rule. If you house two hamsters together, you run the risk of ending up not only with an injured pet, but with an unplanned litter of hamsters.

Physical Condition

Health is of the utmost importance when choosing a hamster. A hamster that is healthy when you first bring him into your home is likely to live to an old age and remain in good health along the way. The opposite is likely true of the hamster that isn't a picture of health at the beginning.

When evaluating potential pets, look for the hamster with sparkling, lively eyes; clean ears held erect and alert; even, well-formed, well-trimmed incisors (the sign of a proper bite and healthy gnawing habits); and a proportioned, compact, barrel-shaped physique that exudes an aura of health.

Stress, diet and general care are also indicated by the condition of the hamster's coat. A healthy hamster's coat should have even fur and be clean (from his incessant self-grooming sessions), with no evidence of hair loss in a young hamster (some hair loss can be normal in an aging hamster). Even though the animal may not be inclined to climb right into your hand in the spirit of "love at first sight," the animal should demonstrate a fun-loving curiosity about his environment—especially about toys.

If you visit the hamster at noon and he seems rather listless and tired, don't simply assume that this lazy little animal obviously isn't the pet for you. Remember that this is a nocturnal creature that would rather be sleeping than impressing would-be owners at this time of day. Come back later in the afternoon or evening to witness his true character.

One thing to avoid is a hamster with a wet rear end. This is not likely caused by the hamster sitting in his water dish! The hamster may be afflicted by the severe bacterial hamster ailment, wet tail. If caught early, this can be treated with antibiotics and fluid therapy, but knowingly choosing a pet with the condition, and perhaps exposing other hamsters that you already own , can spell trouble, as wet tail is highly contagious. Avoid purchasing any other hamsters from the same enclosure as they too may be affected.

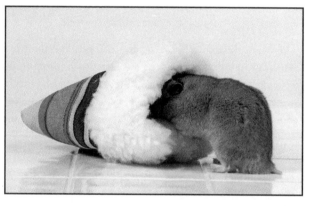

Curiosity is a good indicator of a healthy hamster.

Evaluate the hamster's environment as well. Stress can take a heavy toll on a hamster's health. You may not notice any outward signs of health problems in the hamster from a crowded, unclean enclosure, but a pet coming from such an environment will probably not live as long as one from a clean, stress-free habitat.

What Makes the Hamster Unique?

Indeed the hamster is unique among rodent pets. Consider some of the hamster's cousins, beginning with mice and rats. The hamster does not have centuries behind him of living in close proximity to humans (his history, as we have seen, is quite the opposite), yet despite this distinct difference, mice and rats actually have much in common with their hamster cousins.

Being rodents, mice, rats and hamsters all share chisel-like incisors that require constant gnawing for proper maintenance, all thrive under similar living situations in captivity and eat the same basic diet. Mice, however, tend to be more timid than hamsters and rats, the latter two enjoying regular forays out of their cages with their human handlers—an activity that can prove frightening, even fatally stressful, for most mice. By the same token, hamsters are less gregarious and, with all due respect, not quite as intelligent as rats. Prospective owners seeking an easy-care rodent pet should therefore have a clear vision of what they are looking for in a rodent pet, and what they would rather avoid.

A stress-free environment, including a separate cage and a compassionate owner, is important to a hamster's health.

The major difference between mice and rats and the hamster is an unexpected characteristic that has nothing to do with lifestyle or cohabitation. Yet for some would-be rodent owners this characteristic elevates the hamster instantly above the mouse and rat as the superior pet. That trait is the tail, or, more specifically, the hamster's lack thereof.

For all practical purposes, the pet hamster has no tail. Instead he has a short, tapered stub that contributes to the compact, cylindrical shape of the hamster's physique. This stubby rear end, the product of an underground burrowing existence, has helped kids convince mom and dad to grant permission for a rodent pet. One look at that little creature *sans* tail next to the rats and mice in the pet shop and parents find themselves saying yes to the hamster.

Of course there is more to the hamster than the lack of a tail. Once new owners get past the tail issue, they discover a small pet with a gentle, sweet temperament (if properly handled and socialized), coupled with an appearance that sets him apart as a unique individual among rodent pets.

This individuality is most vividly reflected in the hamster's face and head. His senses of smell and hearing have been largely responsible for the hamster's survival in his native territory. The hamster's eyes are large and expressive, complementing his pink button nose and perky rounded ears that are perched erect, yet slightly askew, at the top of the head.

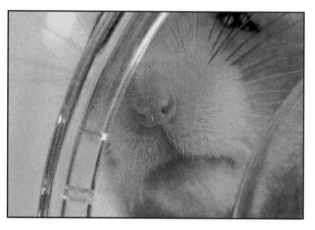

The hamster's button nose is a favorite trait.

The combination of these sensory characteristics lend the hamster a distinct expression of whimsy and fun. Hence the hamster is seen as more cute than he is beautiful. The hamster's chubby, almost jowly, cheeks engineered for food storage invite caricature as does his habit of sitting up on his hind legs, munching on a treat that he holds in his delicate, surprisingly dexterous hands. Most devoted owners could gaze upon such an idyllic scene for hours.

part two
Living with a

Hamster

Bringing
Your Hamster
Home

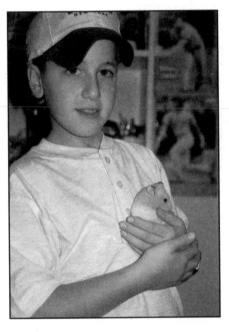

Making Preparations

Once you have decided that the hamster is the pet for you, some preparations are necessary. Purchasing a hamster on impulse because you spot a darling little cream-colored teddy bear that wiggles her whiskers at you as you pass by a pet shop is not the wise way to go. Before you take the plunge, take some time to think about the commitment you would be making, even to what is a relatively inexpensive pet, and carry on with that commitment in mind.

The first step, once you have determined to share your life for the next three years or so with a hamster, is to take stock of what you will need to provide a safe and secure home for your pet. You will need to assemble her habitat (see

Chapter 4, "Housing Your Hamster"); stock up on food; and purchase bedding, food and water receptacles as well as a selection of toys and exercise equipment. Then you will have to decide where to place your hamster's habitat.

Leaving the environment to which she has become accustomed can be a dangerously stressful experience for a hamster. Ease your hamster's anxiety by taking care of the details long before you bring your new pet home.

Hamsters are cute, inexpensive, take little space and are easy to keep clean.

If the hamster is destined for a home with children, which is the norm for this animal that is considered a wonderful children's pet, by all means involve the kids in the preparation process, but remember that a hamster must never be relegated to the sole care of a child. While these easy-care pets provide kids with a fine opportunity to learn and experience the responsibility of caring for a helpless creature, even the most dependable kids have been known to sleep on the job from time to time. Parents must remain involved to ensure that the hamster continues to receive the optimum care she requires.

Finally, enjoy the anticipation. Working together, purchasing the equipment, preparing a new pet's home, learning the ins and outs of proper care—there are few joys in life more thrilling for kids and adults alike. Take it slow, proceed with

common sense and you are sure to make the arrival of your
new pet a truly memorable experience for the entire family.

Quality Veterinary Services

Before you bring your new pet home, you should take the
time to find a veterinarian. Ask other hamster owners for
references, then visit two or three clinics to get a feel for the
practice. You need to find a veterinarian who has experience,

*Get to know the
special character-
istics of your new
hamster, includ-
ing requirements
for physical exer-
cise and mental
stimulation.*

equipment, drugs and a trained staff for small animals. This
includes a working knowledge of diseases and responses to
medications that hamsters may have, as well as dietary
needs, behavior and reproduction. Along with this level of
expertise, look for the availability of emergency or after-
hours service. Your hamster will
benefit from a veterinarian who
is familiar and comfortable
with treating the medical problems of small and exotic animals. The first stop before you
take your new hamster home
should be a visit to the veterinarian so you can get a baseline
evaluation of the hamster's
health.

Welcoming Your
New Pet Home

Common sense should prevail
when that grand day arrives.
You are ready to pick up your
pet and bring her home. The
habitat is clean and organized,
fresh food and water await, a
layer of clean bedding sits ready to invite the attentions of a
burrowing little creature, and the toys are ready for play.

This day provides you with the ideal time to begin earning
your new hamster's respect. Work toward this ultimate goal

from your first meeting, and you just might be rewarded with a bond between pet and owner that you find quite surprising.

When you pick up your hamster, bring a small ventilated container with you for transport of your new pet. Most stores will have these available, but again, you want to be prepared. If the trip will be a short one (which is preferable), a heavy cardboard box with holes for ventilation will suffice. But to prevent the hamster from attempting an escape by chewing, a heavier plastic, also well-ventilated container may be superior. This latter item will also come in handy down the road as a "holding pen" for the hamster when you are cleaning her cage.

Pictured are travel supplies for your hamster: a well-ventilated container, food and water, bedding and some toys.

Place some bedding material in this small travel box—if possible some bedding from the hamster's enclosure at the pet shop, shelter or breeding facility—to provide not only a comfortable ride, but a familiar scent, as well. Stash a couple of treats in your pocket, too, perhaps a peanut in the shell or a sunflower seed to offer your new pet and keep her occupied for the journey home.

After visiting the veterinarian, take the hamster directly to her new home. Don't stop off at a party first or visit a child's classroom to show off the new pet. Keep the animal's well-being and the alleviation of her stress in mind. Your job is to get your hamster home as soon as possible, place her in her new home, and then leave her alone for a while to get accustomed to her surroundings.

Assuming you have already wisely placed the hamster's habitat in a quiet, untraveled corner of the house, once home, the hamster will probably explore the new enclosure a bit, check out her food, and perhaps burrow into some shavings for a little nap to recover from the journey. Providing the hamster with the opportunity to partake of these simple introductory acts is your first step toward earning your new pet's lifelong respect.

Gentle Hamster Handling

Take your time in interacting with your new hamster. Even if she seems ready for play, introduce yourself gradually. You will both benefit in the long run.

Hamsters navigate through their world by relying primarily on their senses of smell and hearing. During your first few days together, allow her to get acquainted with your voice and your scent. Do this by speaking softly to the hamster when you approach her enclosure for daily feedings, water changes, toy rotations (just like children, hamsters thrive with an ever-changing variety of playthings) and the daily removal of soiled bedding.

All the family members can introduce themselves this way, but try to keep your brief interactions to a minimum. Do your hamster a favor and reserve these interactions only for the animal's family members in the beginning. The kids may be tempted to invite everyone in the neighborhood over to meet the family's new hamster, but explain that it's better to wait a few days to let her get adjusted to her immediate family. Once you build that important foundation of respect, the hamster should be amenable to meeting outsiders—and probably friendlier in doing so, as well.

When you believe the hamster is ready for you to do so, gently reach your hand into her habitat, an act that will invite the animal to approach and sniff your skin. If treated gently, most hamsters are not biters by nature. If your new pet tries to take a little nip of your finger while exploring your hand, either she isn't ready for such an intrusion or she may have caught a whiff of your lunch lingering on your fingertips.

You will further earn your hamster's esteem by reserving these initial interactions to the late afternoon and early evening when this nocturnal creature shakes off her daytime sleepiness and emerges energetic and ready for activity. If you awaken the animal constantly during the day when she is trying to sleep, the hamster will likely become frustrated with this new, and rather inconsiderate, human in her life. Waking a soundly sleeping hamster, even one known for a docile disposition, could incite a bite that must not be blamed on hamster nastiness, but owner negligence and disrespect.

Wrap your fingers gently but confidently around the hamster's body, then lift her out of the cage.

Holding Your Hamster

After those first few days of quiet introductions, your hamster is ready for the next step—being handled. Proceed gradually. Before lifting the hamster out of her enclosure, speak softly to alert her to your presence. Next, gently place your hand into her enclosure as she has become accustomed to your doing.

While technically hamsters can be lifted by the excess skin at the napes of their necks, it is better to simply wrap your fingers gently yet firmly around her barrel-shaped body and lift her up. Use your other hand to offer extra support at the hamster's rear end and hold the animal close to your body.

If your hamster loves to speed around the cage and dart out of your grasp, try this tip: Create a wall by putting the palms of your hands together, and the hamster will generally run into the wall, letting you close your hands around her body.

During initial outings and whenever children handle the hamster, make sure the hamster is held close over a surface such as a table or the floor to prevent injuries if she falls. By the same token, never leave the hamster alone on a table or elevated surface. To do so is to invite disaster for your pet who, due to her insatiable curiosity, could be seriously injured.

Always look for physical changes in your hamster.

Handling your hamster with respect and a quiet demeanor will instill in the animal a sense of security and positive association with being handled and, as an offshoot, toward her new human family members. Your pet will recognize when she is being treated with respect and will learn quickly whom she may trust. Introduce yourself gradually and gently, observe those preliminary safety precautions when handling the animal, and you will earn a trustworthy reputation.

Hamster Habits

First-time hamster owners are usually surprised at all there is
to learn about the species when a hamster joins the family.
Much of this can be learned simply by observing the hamster and heeding her signals.

Grooming

Watch your hamster regularly and you will soon realize that
this little animal grooms herself constantly. Before eating,
after eating, before a nap, after a
nap, before a spin in the hamster
ball, after a spin in the hamster
ball—the hamster stops, straight-
ens any displaced hairs, and washes
her face for the seventeenth time
that day. Indeed this is a meticulously clean little pet, so diligent
about cleanliness, both her own
and her habitat's, that she could be
christened the Felix Unger of the
rodent world.

Though some owners may view
such habits as a sign that the hamster requires grooming by her owners, that is an incorrect notion.
The hamster is perfectly capable of
taking care of her own grooming,
no doubt a skill sculpted by her solitary life in the wild
where, in the absence of other hamsters to join in sessions of
mutual grooming, the hamster learned to groom on her
own. This has more to do with survival than with vanity, as
a healthy coat is critical to protecting the hamster from cli-
mactic extremes.

*Grooming the
hamster with a
soft brush helps
remove bedding
dust and is a
great way to bond
with your pet.*

As a rule, hamsters should not be bathed. Because their
grooming routines serve to cleanse them naturally—and
because they are essentially odorless by nature—there is no
need for a human-style bath. Owners should forego bathing
their hamster because bathing can be too stressful; that stress

can lead to a sick hamster. Hamsters are especially prone to respiratory problems, so it is best to avoid the potential chill a bath can cause, which, when combined with the stress of the experience, can cause illness.

If you still feel inclined to assist your hamster in her grooming regimen, you can do so by brushing the animal gently with a soft toothbrush. Most hamsters are amenable to short brushing sessions that can also help remove bedding dust or other habitat residue that may cling to the hair.

Housing
Your Hamster

When it comes to home, hamsters are determined homebodies, never content unless they are living in the ultimate hamster domicile with everything in its place and all corners squeaky clean. Yet the hamster, even the happy hamster, is the consummate escape artist. Escape is seen as a grand game, reminiscent of what sent wild hamsters over miles and miles of desert terrain in search of food and adventure. The challenge is to place your hamster in an enclosure with-

out even the tiniest possible escape route—such as an ill-fitting top or a tiny hole that can be gnawed.

Hamster Habitats

The goal of the hamster owner, is to provide the hamster with a home so attractive, well-furnished and clean, that the animal won't need to entertain the possibility of escape. The good news is that meeting this goal is quite simple.

The ideal hamster habitat has separate areas for sleeping and eating, a bathroom and play space.

The important elements to understand in optimum hamster housing is that this animal requires cleanliness as well as neatness. He will only rest when everything within his environment is arranged with a distinct spot for eating, drinking, and sleeping; another section for playing; and another designated as a bathroom. Consequently, the rule of thumb in hamster housing is that bigger is better.

Various types of housing exist for these animals, and opinions vary widely on which is best. But all veteran hamster keepers agree that one should strive to provide the hamster with as much room as possible, at least 19 square inches. A roomy enclosure offers you the opportunity to design the interior with all the separate areas for the hamster's various life functions.

Set up the hamster's home before ever bringing your new pet home—set up the sleeping area, the bathroom, the eating and play areas and cover the floor with bedding.

The Glass or Plastic Aquarium-Style Tank

A popular setup for hamster keeping—and one in which you will most often find pets displayed—is the glass aquarium. (A variation on this is a plastic version that comes fully equipped with a ventilated handle top and other internal accessories.) For a single hamster, the aquarium tank should be at least 10 gallons in size, it must be well constructed (no sharp edges at the corners, no cracked sides) and it must have a well-fitting top with no gaps or holes that can inspire escape.

The best top for an aquarium setup is a closely meshed screen top framed with metal that slides on and off. This type ensures not only security—the hamster, skilled as he may be, cannot slide the properly installed top off—but it also provides ventilation, which is critical to hamster health.

Another style of tank setup provides even more ventilation because it boasts a screen top as well as one side of screen. The mesh of the screening on any hamster home must be woven closely enough to prevent the injury of tiny hamster toes, and it must be free of tears that could be enlarged by a hamster bent on escape.

The benefits of aquarium-style housing are that it is easy to clean; keeps odors at bay; and retains hay, bedding, food and residual dust within the hamster's house (and prevents it from overwhelming yours). Furthermore, if the enclosure is properly roofed, this style of hamster home keeps the hamster safe and confined, yet quite visible to the many admirers who will want to come and observe the little fellow as he plays, eats and naps.

Hamsters are opportunistic escape artists and it is wise to check your pet's enclosure frequently for escape possibilities.

The owner should be aware that there can be a potential lack of ventilation with this tank. In other words, because it is enclosed, the owner must check the cleanliness frequently as there will not be an odor that indicates it's cleaning time. The tank may prevent the dissemination of odors throughout the household at large, but it must be cleaned often to maintain the hamster's health.

An aquarium tank should be at least 10 gallons in size, with no sharp edges at the corners, no cracked sides and a well-fitting top with no gaps or holes.

The Traditional Wire Cage

While countless hamster keepers swear by the aquarium style hamster house, there are just as many who would choose nothing other than a traditional wire cage. Ventilation, they claim, is the number one reason for doing so, and indeed a roomy, airy enclosure helps prevent respiratory illness in resident hamsters.

As with any choice of hamster domicile, the cage must be well made and free of exposed wires or tears that could lead to injury and/or escape. The floor should be solid to hold in bedding and to facilitate burrowing, and the door should be one that can be latched securely. Even though this design is obviously light and airy, this does not mean that you may forego the routine cleaning. Any style of housing must be cleaned regularly (more on how to go about that later), and the wire cage is no exception.

One trend in cages that is best avoided is the double-decker design. While such a setup is considered ideal for the hamster's larger cousin, the chinchilla, it can prove dangerous for the small hamster, which is not as adept at climbing (he is a burrower, after all). He could take a serious tumble from the higher reaches of such a cage. Stick with the traditional single-story design and make life safer for your pet.

Tube Setups

Although it is often referred to generically as a Habitrail, there are various brands of this unique hamster setup that imitate the hamster's natural underground environment. The setup is a configuration of plastic tubes, compartments and similar segments that an owner assembles in various arrangements, enabling the hamster to climb through a maze not all that different from the vast burrows and tunnels hamsters inhabit in the wild.

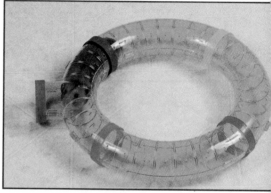

This setup is a delightfully fun environment for a hamster because it satisfies the small rodent's natural instincts to burrow and travel through narrow tunnels, but it has drawbacks as well. Cleaning, for one, can be a challenge, in that the unit must be disassembled to clean the various segments thoroughly—and reassembled once cleaning is done. Failure to clean it properly results in an overpowering smell from urine and bits of food left in the various reaches of the habitat.

Some owners prefer to keep their hamster in a traditional tank and provide external tubes for a playtime treat.

Another drawback is that hamsters have been known to chew through the plastic of these systems, which can obviously cause a variety of problems. The hamster can escape, he can suffer digestive upset and the results of his efforts can prove economically costly to the owner.

Many hamster owners have devised a compromise, in which the tube setup is used not as a hamster's primary residence, but as a supplement to the primary residence. In this way, the hamster can eat and sleep in his more traditional cage or tank, and then enjoy playtime in the tube habitat. Such a combination provides the hamster—and his owner—with the best of both worlds.

Homemade Enclosures

Most veteran hamster keepers recommend that owners steer clear of homemade hamster habitats. Unless you are an expert on rodent behavior and physiology and how these animals interact with various materials they might find in their environment, you are wise to rely on those who are, and choose a commercially made product that will prove to be safer and more secure for the hamster.

Commercial enclosures of gnaw-proof glass, metal or wire are superior to a homemade wooden structure—and less expensive in the long run. Stick with the more traditional setups, and avoid any unexpected, not to mention easily prevented, tragedies.

Bedding material, food and water containers, treats (such as sunflower seeds), an exercise wheel and toys are some essentials for the hamster cage.

Additional Supplies

There is far more to the ideal hamster habitat than walls alone. The furnishings within those walls are just as vital to keeping the hamster healthy and mentally stimulated.

There are several items that you'll want to have on hand before you bring your hamster home: a water bottle or dish, a food dish, nesting/bedding material, an exercise wheel and/or ball and some toys. You also need to have a supply of food ready for your new friend as discussed in chapter 5.

Water Bottle

Hamsters need to have fresh water available at all times. Pet stores sell various sizes of water bottles, it is recommended to keep a medium-size bottle in your hamster's cage. To ensure that the water is always fresh you should change the water in the bottle daily. When you clean the bottle, be sure that it is well rinsed of all traces of soap. If the bottle gets too dirty, it is time to get a new one. Some hamsters like to use a water dish, but end up sitting it the water and dirtying it or tip the dish over altogether.

There are several types of bird dishes available that fasten securely to the side of the cage. Using this type of dish will help prevent your hamster from tipping his water, but you must make sure that the dish is fastened low enough for the hamster to reach. Some owners place the water dish directly under the water bottle to catch drips and prevent soaked bedding.

Food Dishes

Hamsters tend to enjoy sitting in their food dishes as well as eating from them, so a weighted dish is recommended. The bowl that you get for your hamster should be large enough to hold an ample supply of food for their daily energy needs. Make sure the dish is shallow enough that your hamster can reach the food at the bottom.

Bedding

The choice and type of bedding you choose for your hamster is crucial to his well-being. This is, after all, a burrowing animal that takes great pleasure in digging into a mound of bedding for a nap, for a game or for hiding a litter of newborns. Your choice of bedding is not only directly connected to the hamster's pleasure in this, but also to his overall health.

While hamsters are burrowing animals, this does not mean you need to recreate his natural environment in your home. Avoid the temptation to carpet the floor of the hamster's enclosure with a thick layer of natural materials through which he can burrow and build his own maze of tunnels. These materials can actually prove to be *too* natural, containing parasites, bacteria and other disease-carrying agents that could prove deadly to the resident hamster.

Bedding should be clean, dry, nontoxic and absorbent. The most popular bedding choice, and one that typically satisfies this criteria, is wood shavings. Avoid cedar shavings, as this aromatic wood can prove too intense to small rodents. Opt instead for pine or aspen. These must be shavings that are produced specifically for the care of small animals; don't carpet the enclosure with remnants from a lumber yard or woodworking shop. The hamster can suffer severe repercussions from the dust and chemicals in the wood. Similar problems can arise from cat litter, another inappropriate bedding choice for hamsters.

Nesting material should be clean, dry and non-toxic—covering 2 to 3 inches of the habitat floor.

Other bedding options include products made from vegetable materials and shredded paper. Should you choose the paper option, avoid newspaper. The ink can be toxic. Plain, unprinted newspaper stock or another type of similarly plain paper is a better option.

You may supplement the bedding with a few handfuls of hay. Like everything you place in your hamster's habitat, the hay, too, must be clean, dry and free of parasites and mold. Place the hay in one section of the enclosure to designate the nesting area.

Regardless of the type you choose, cover the floor of the hamster's habitat with 2 or 3 inches of clean, fresh bedding. This will provide your pet with ample room in which to burrow, play and hide. If you carpet the floor with a generous layer of bedding and keep it clean, you're maintaining a sound foundation for all other furnishings in the hamster's abode.

Hideaways (Nest Boxes)

As a nocturnal creature—and as a small rodent—the hamster must have somewhere to hide from the prying eyes of his admirers. Provide your pet with a variety of beds in which he can build a cozy nest.

The choice of these items must be made with hamster physiology in mind. Remember those teeth and their shredding ability, and keep away from any materials that could fall victim to chewing. Soft plastic and cardboard, for example, won't last long with a hamster about. Hard plastic, PVC piping and the various items made specifically for hamster habitats are superior choices—and less expensive in the long run because they don't need to be constantly replaced.

Position one or two of these nest boxes in the hamster's home—preferably some distance away from the food dishes and the water bottle, as these should occupy their own specific spots within the habitat. The hamster tends to designate a particular corner of his domicile as a bathroom. Once you figure out just where this is, position food, water and nest boxes away from that area, and foster the hamster's desire for order and cleanliness.

As for the nest/hiding boxes themselves, a variety of styles exist. You may want to provide your hamster with two choices to offer him a bit of variety. Your hamster may enjoy, for example, one box with solid walls in which he can hide completely from the outside world, and another with clear hard plastic walls and several different openings that he can use as a makeshift playhouse.

The best nest hideaways are those that provide the hamster with an accessible door opening and plenty of privacy once the hamster is inside, some of which are available commercially (you may find smaller models for dwarf hamsters as these are becoming more popular). Some of these are traditional box shapes, and others come in a variety of styles, designs and shapes to keep a hamster interested and entertained. Most commercial styles are composed of safe, nontoxic materials that can withstand long-term rodent gnawing.

Some household items can also be used as hamster hideaways—although these are usually temporary because of the materials involved. An empty tissue box or cylindrical oatmeal container, for example, can provide the hamster with a fun change of pace, but because these items are made of cardboard, they probably won't last long. Use your imagination when seeking out household items for your pet, but always keep the basic rules of hamster safety in mind.

Alternating different shaped toys gives the hamster something new to explore and climb on.

Proper Toys

Hamsters are very active and thrive on stimulation. They enjoy interactions both with their owners and new and exciting items within their environment.

Offer your pet a variety of toys, all of which must be well-constructed and made of nontoxic materials. The classic hamster toy is the exercise wheel, but running on the wheel can be addictive, not to mention noisy for the owner when the hamster runs all night. By all means give your hamster a wheel to run on, but offer him other toys as well.

Supplement the wheel with several other toys. The hamster ball—a hollow plastic ball into which a hamster may securely sit and "run" through the house safely—is a favorite, as are commercially available ladders, bridges and novelty hideaways that may be used for hiding and climbing. A variety of common household items are also available for play purposes, such as cardboard toilet paper or paper towel rolls and remnants of PVC piping, both of which the hamster may use for a rousing game of hide-and-seek.

This hamster car is a great variation of the exercise ball.

Fruit tree branches and chunks of wood for gnawing are also fun for the hamster and at the same time attractive additions to the hamster habitat. They not only provide the animal with a new and different surface on which to climb, but also a delectable gnawing item. To protect the hamster, make sure that the wood or branch is clean, untreated and nontoxic. You can buy pieces from well-stocked pet supply stores.

Safety should as always be first on your mind when choosing hamster toys. Make sure the toys are the right size for your hamster, such as smaller hamster balls and wheels for dwarfs and larger items for goldens. Check the wheel regularly, too, to ensure it remains in good working order, with no exposed wires or sharp edges that could hurt the toes or tummy of a particularly athletic hamster, or catch the long hair of a teddy bear hamster.

When placing new toys within your hamster's abode (which you should do periodically, replacing familiar items with new exciting ones and rotating the toys every day or two to retain your pet's interest), make sure the toys sit securely in the flooring material so as not to roll over or fall onto a hamster should he use it in a way that was not intended.

Household Upkeep

Regardless of the particular housing you choose, your pet's home must be cleaned regularly and thoroughly. A clean cage will keep your hamster happy and active as well as in good health.

First, soiled bedding should be removed daily from the enclosure, which is typically quite simple because most hamsters will designate one specific corner of their enclosure as the bathroom. Simply remove the affected material and you have done your job.

Hamster Toys

Exercise wheel

Hamster ball

Play ladders and bridges

Varied toys for climbing

Cardboard cylinders

PVC piping

Uneaten food should also be removed each day, which may prove a bit more of a challenge. It's not unusual for a hamster with an excess of food to fill his ample cheek pouches and bury his treasure somewhere within the bedding, perhaps in his nest box or beneath a favorite toy. If your hamster has this traditional habit, try to find his cache, clean it out, and thus prevent a buildup of odor from the natural decomposition of food.

In addition to daily maintenance, the bedding should be completely removed and replaced every week. When it comes time to do this, place the resident hamster in an established holding cage or box—a small, secure enclosure equipped with a bit of bedding and a toy or two as well as some food for the hamster's comfort (you can also use this holding cage for trips to the veterinarian or for family travels). As with the main enclosure, make sure the holding cage is clean and escape-proof.

With your hamster safely confined and out of the way, carry on with the cleaning. Remove all the items from the cage, and clean everything with warm water and mild soap or detergent. Dispose of the bedding from the enclosure, and thoroughly clean the walls and the floor (or the segments of the tube setup) with warm water and mild soap. Avoid strong detergents or cleaning solvents that can irritate the hamster's respiratory tract or prove to be toxic if not completely rinsed away. Rinse the soap from the enclosure thoroughly—you want to be rid of every bit of soap residue—and then dry the surfaces just as thoroughly.

Thorough cleaning of your hamster's cage every week is essential to maintaining the health and wellbeing of your pet.

Once the enclosure is dry, carpet the floor with a new fresh 2- or 3-inch layer of bedding, replace the cage furnishings and, finally, replace the resident hamster.

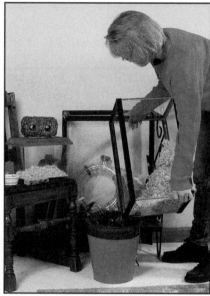

Where to Place the Habitat?

Basic maintenance of your hamster's habitat is critical, but so is the placement of that enclosure. First, the hamster must reside indoors. Since the wild hamster spent a great deal of time underground, the hamster simply does not do well exposed to the elements, especially when those elements involve extreme temperatures, precipitation and the threat of unwelcome visitors. A layer of bedding will not suffice in keeping the hamster protected from these elements, so keep him indoors where he will remain physically safe and emotionally secure.

Hamster Nightlife

The nocturnal nature of the hamster should be kept in mind when you decide where to place the habitat within your house. The hamster that is allowed to follow his own natural rhythms will sleep during the day and play at night. Therefore, place his enclosure in a section of the house that is quiet, dimly lit and protected from the traffic of the family's daily activities.

When the hamster awakens full of energy and ready to play in the afternoon or early evening, make sure he has toys and food to enjoy. This is also the perfect opportunity for you to take the hamster out of his enclosure for some interactions with his family or for a romp in his tube habitat.

As the evening progresses, you must also think of your own sleep patterns. You can remedy the squeaking wheel situation—and ensure you get a good night's sleep yourself—by placing the hamster's cage far enough away from your own sleeping area, and providing the animal with a variety of toys so he doesn't become addicted to the wheel.

Temperature Requirements

Limit the stress your hamster may experience from the attention of other household pets.

The enclosure should remain safely out of direct sunlight at all times. Heat and exposure to direct sun can be extremely harmful to your hamster's health. When evaluating where your hamster's cage should sit, keep in mind that the sunlight will change during the day, so a shaded spot by a window in the morning could be flooded with sun in the afternoon.

Avoid drafts, as well, either from open windows or air conditioning vents. Drafts are particularly dangerous to hamsters, as they can contribute to respiratory problems. The ideal draft-free temperature for hamsters is anywhere from 65 to 80 degrees Fahrenheit (for newborn hamsters the ideal temperature is 70 to 75 degrees). Though they are desert dwellers by nature, they thrive best in the same basic room temperatures preferred by humans.

Hamster-Proofing

Make sure that no particularly dangerous household items are within reach of the cage, and thus the hamster, either. You certainly don't want electrical cords hanging into the enclosure that could be inviting to the hamster's gnawing habits, nor do you want your pet's home to be situated near cleaning solvents or similar chemical agents with fumes that could prove damaging to the hamster's sensitive respiratory tract.

Finally, make sure the enclosure is in a safe place. He should be situated out of the reach of other household pets, such a cats and dogs, that may not be able to physically harm the hamster, but whose mere presence outside of the enclosure is enough to cause stress.

Feeding
Your Hamster

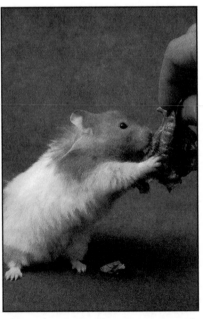

The ease with which one can provide a hamster with a healthy, well-balanced diet is one of the reasons this animal is considered such an easy-care pet. Though she requires access to her food at all times, supplying that food is so simple even a young child can take on the duty (with parental supervision, of course).

Nutritional Needs

While we are inclined to think of the hamster as the quintessential vegetarian, in the wild the hamster enjoys a quite variegated—and rather omnivorous—diet. In addition to feasting on the vegetation products she finds during her nightly forays into her desert environment, she may supplement her diet with insects and any other meat-based items she happens to find.

48

Vegetarian Diet?

Many hamster owners acquire these animals because of their classically vegetarian diets, and you, the owner of the domestic hamster, need not mimic the carnivorous aspect of the wild hamster's diet by supplying your pet with meat or insects. To satisfy the hamster's daily protein needs, in which proteins should comprise approximately 15 to 20 percent of the diet, some hamster keepers promote the idea that you can supplement the animal's diet with mealworms. This is not necessary, however, and can actually cause digestive problems for the species that far outweigh any nutritional benefits mealworms present—nutritional benefits that can be garnered far easier from other food sources.

A safer and easier method of supplying hamsters with animal-based protein is to offer the animals a bit of cooked meat from time to time, but even this is not a necessary component of the healthy hamster diet. Feel free to offer your hamster a classically vegetarian diet, but be sure to vary what you feed her.

> ### Feeding Your Hamster
>
> Feeding your hamster is a simple task, just follow the guidelines and ask your veterinarian if you have any concerns.
>
> - varied diet consisting of a mix of commercially prepared food and fresh vegetables
> - food available at all times
> - constant supply of fresh, clean water
> - healthful treats in moderation

The Basic Components

Like all mammals, the hamster requires a balanced diet composed of the basic nutrients: carbohydrates, fats, proteins, vitamins, minerals and plenty of fresh, clean water. The most efficient way to supply your pet with these nutrients is in a diet that combines commercially prepared hamster foods that are readily available at pet supply stores with fresh foods that are readily available in your own kitchen.

Commercial Diets

Thanks to the popularity of pocket pets and the knowledge of their nutritional needs, there are a variety of commercial products on the market that please both the hamster's palate and the owner's desire for convenient feeding practices.

Basic seed mixtures are the first and more traditional of the commercially prepared foods. Most hamsters are thrilled with a mix of seeds, but if served as the sole dietary source, this will probably not provide the animal with a complete balance of nutrients. If the hamster chooses not to partake of all the ingredients, she will not get a complete balance, even though the mix represents a balanced diet.

It's not at all unusual for a particularly finicky hamster to choose to feast only on sunflower seeds or only on some other type of seed she finds in the mix. Because no one food, especially no one seed, is the perfect food, eating only one component of a balanced diet will lead to malnutrition. If that ingredient happens to be a seed, she is also in danger of obesity, as seeds and nuts are very high in fat. In moderation, they are a fine component of the diet, but they are not appropriate as the sole component.

A basic seed mix should be combined with other foods, such as fresh vegetables, to provide a complete diet for your hamster.

Pelleted or block-type food products are another type of commercial diet that prevents the problems of the seed mixture. Within the pellets and blocks are combined all the nutrients the hamster requires for a complete and balanced diet, and the hamster has no possibility of picking and choosing what she wants to eat and what she doesn't. Many of the block diets present an added bonus: Their hard consistency helps keep the teeth trimmed, maintaining the hamster's dental health while nourishing her at the same time.

Because the seed mixture is generally tastier and more interesting to the hamster than the pelleted and block-type concoctions, the seed mixture is best fed in addition to the pellets or blocks to ensure the hamster both enjoys her meal and receives a proper mix of nutrients. If you happen to have a hamster that prefers seeds, however, you may need to wait to offer the seed mixture until after the hamster has ingested a ration of pellets or blocks.

A block-type food mix is a good way to provide your hamster with necessary nutrients.

In addition to providing a hamster with her complete nutrition, commercial diets are further beneficial in that they are readily available at most pet supply stores and they can be easily stored. Resist the temptation to stock up on these foods, however, because even though they boast relatively long shelf lives, they can still go bad.

When purchased in modest amounts and stored correctly—preferably in plastic airtight containers with secure lids—commercial hamster food should remain fresh and clean for weeks. If, however, you notice the supply has become moldy, stale or otherwise less than ideal, do not offer it to your hamster. Dispose of the supply and replace it with a fresh batch.

Fresh foods can also help keep your pet interested in her food, and thus help ensure she receives a full, well-balanced complement of nutrients. Most hamsters love nothing more than to go to the food dish and find a small helping of chopped, fresh vegetables, such as broccoli, parsley, carrots or perhaps a couple of peas. Tiny chunks of cheese, pasta or whole wheat bread, and an occasional morsel of apple or orange, can also be added to the diet.

These foods, fed sparingly, must be fresh. They should be of the same quality you would demand of your own diet. Feeding your hamster a few tiny bites of fresh food each day helps to round out the diet and to keep the hamster interested in eating. However, feeding her leftovers could result in gastric upset and obesity.

Remember that even the freshest of foods won't stay that way for long, so the uneaten portions must be removed each day to prevent spoilage. Of special concern from a sanitary standpoint is that these foods are certain to spoil if stored with a hamster's hidden supply, which is where many a hamster is apt to deliver the leftovers when mealtime is over. Keep track of what fresh foods you offer your pet, and how much you feed. If the daily ration seems to have disappeared too quickly, search for a stash of food that will be prone to spoilage after a couple of days.

Fresh vegetables and fruits including bits of apples and oranges, lettuce, carrots, broccoli and parsley should be served to your hamster on a daily basis.

Treats should be healthful and offered to your hamster in moderation. Appropriate and highly coveted hamster treats include raisins, peanuts in the shell, a small bite of fruit and various commercially prepared treats that contain a variety of natural ingredients.

Regardless of what type of treats you choose, they must be offered sparingly so as not to interfere with the balance of the hamster's primary diet or cause gastric upset or obesity.

Treats should not be viewed as an everyday event, nor should they be considered part of the basic diet. Treats can be lifesavers, particularly when a hamster escapes from her cage or disappears from where she is playing in the living room.

Water occupies a most prominent spot on the list of vital nutrients and is in fact the one component that binds all the others together.

Without fresh, clean water every day, the hamster's system—or any mammal's—will be completely unable to operate. Each and every cell within the body requires water to function and to reproduce.

It is no surprise that without ample amounts of water in her system, an animal's blood cannot flow correctly, her organs cannot carry out their jobs, and her brain cannot function as it should. A lack of water (typically caused either by an empty water bottle or dish, an illness that causes her not to drink or by diarrhea) leads to dehydration, which in turn may lead to death. This can be easily prevented, of course, by supplying your small pet with fresh, clean water in squeaky clean containers every day—and monitoring how much she drinks.

> **Treats Can Be Lifesavers**
>
> One way to find an escaped and soon-to-be-hungry hamster is to entice her out into the open by baiting each room with her favored treats. After setting traps—say, a handful of raisins in every room— the owner usually will walk into a room of the house where he or she least expects to spot the hamster, and finds his or her pet sitting up on her haunches, nibbling contentedly on a raisin she holds securely in her delicate fingers.

How to Feed a Hamster

Once you understand the simple components of the optimum hamster diet, you must design a feeding regimen. This, not surprisingly, is just as simple as the diet itself.

The hamster is a rodent with a speedy metabolism. She must have access to food at all times to feed those ample energy needs. Although the hamster will typically eat most of her daily rations during the night, she must have food available during the day should she awaken and need a midday snack.

Food Dishes

If feeding the hamster in a traditional dish, the food is best offered in a heavy ceramic bowl, weighted at the bottom to prevent her from tipping it over and leaving a mess of food and bedding on the cage floor. Nest the dish securely within the bedding of the enclosure to prevent spillage, and place it some distance from the hamster's nest box and from her designated bathroom area. In the hamster's mind, there's a distinct place for every thing and every thing must be in its place.

If you have a problem with the food being soiled in an open air dish situated in the middle of the enclosure—perhaps by a hamster who's favorite place to sit is inside her food dish—there are dish styles available that can clamp on to a cage wall. Such a dish must sit low enough to the floor of the habitat to make it easily accessible to the hamster.

Hamsters are playful, avid exercisers with a very fast metabolism. Care should be taken to provide ample food during the day and especially at night, when they are most active.

Another option is a block-type diet administered from receptacles that hang from the enclosure wall (which must also be placed low enough for the hamster to reach). But this latter option requires the presence of an additional food dish for seed mixture, if it is being offered, and any fresh foods the hamster will be eating that day.

Water Containers

Fresh water should given each day, preferably in a water bottle mounted to the side of the enclosure with a metal sipping tube (avoid plastic tubes that can be chewed and destroyed by a hamster's gnawing). The bottle should be emptied and refilled daily with a fresh supply of water, and the sipping tube must be checked every day, too, for possible blockages that would prevent the hamster from drinking properly and getting the fluid her body needs.

You might also offer water in a heavy ceramic dish identical to the type you use for the food dish, but this is a far messier alternative and not one that is considered ideal for hamsters. Aside from the fact that the dish can become soiled with food, dust, bedding and feces as it sits exposed to the open air and the hamster's activities, there is also the danger that the water dish will spill, leaving the hamster without drinking water and a habitat floor carpeted with soaked bedding.

Check your hamster's water bottle daily to see that she is drinking enough.

Regardless of the equipment with which you choose to feed your hamster, all items must be cleaned thoroughly each day. Empty the previous day's contents (food or water), scrub the dish or bottle with a mild soap and warm water (avoid strong detergents and chemical disinfectants) and rinse the item thoroughly to remove all soap residues. If soap remains on the dish or bottle, the hamster could ingest it with her next meal or drink, and subsequently suffer from a nasty bout of gastric upset.

Keeping
Your
Hamster Healthy

As we know, our pets are not immortal. When we choose to live intimately with animals in our homes, we must acknowledge that we will outlive them. Indeed their life spans are far shorter than our own—this is especially true of hamsters that typically live only two to three years.

Although their life spans are short, we are bound by honor to do all we can to make those years as fulfilling and healthy as possible for the animals and to alleviate any suffering they may have. There are steps we can take to help them enjoy the longest lives possible and to foster the lovely bond that can exist between an owner and his or her pet.

Preventive Care

Part of this mission is to observe the hamster for subtle changes that could indicate the early stages of a budding health problem. The medical establishment has long understood that the earlier treatment is sought for an ailment, the greater chance the patient has of recovering successfully. It is up to the animal's owner, the individual who knows the animal best, to look for those early signs. Get to know your pet's physical and behavioral characteristics when he is healthy—the texture and density of his hair; the contour of his skin and physique; the patterns of his eating, sleeping and playing behaviors; and his natural aroma—and you will be better prepared to notice any change that could indicate the first sign of a problem.

Warning Signs

Common Illness   Some of the more common "red flag" changes to look out for are the sudden onset of uncharacteristic lethargy (especially at playtime in the late afternoon and evening); a lack of appetite; diarrhea and/or the presence of moisture around the hamster's rear end (the classic sign of the hamster ailment known as wet tail); a deterioration in the quality, density and texture of the hair (although some loss and thinning of the hair is common with age in a hamster); a swollen abdomen; incessant scratching of the skin; a failure to tend to routine grooming duties; or an unusual odor in what is essentially an odorless animal. These signs could indicate any number of conditions that require medical attention.

Acute Illness   You should also be on the lookout for more complex behaviors and symptoms. A hamster that begins to exhibit circling behavior, for example, may be suffering from an ear infection. Excessive thirst and urination are serious signs that indicate kidney disease, diabetes or adrenal disease. The development of lumps or bumps under the skin could signal the presence of tumors or abscesses, which

> ## Creating a Healthful Environment
>
> Alleviating your hamster's breathing difficulties by altering problem-causing agents within his environment is not only simple, but results in quick and noticeable improvement.
>
> If, for example, you suspect cold temperatures and drafts are to blame for your hamster's noisy breathing, move your pet's enclosure to a spot that is warmer and free from drafts. If bedding dust and oils are a problem, try a pelleted paper or vegetable product and avoid cedar and wood shavings. Your hamster will breathe easier for it.

require veterinary attention. Discharge from the eye is also a cause for concern in hamsters, as they are prone to eye infections. Should such a discharge persist, contact the veterinarian for advice and/or treatment.

The owner who interacts daily with his or her pet hamster and observes him carefully for those telltale signs, will be able to report these observations to the hamster's veterinarian early on. Early treatment and fast action will increase the opportunity for a full recovery from the illness.

Practicing Prevention

More veterinarians today are trained to treat small and exotic pets and encourage owners to bring pocket pets in for routine visits.

At the same time, the owner can further increase those odds—and prevent problems from beginning in the first place—by adopting responsible hamster keeping practices. For example, feed your hamster a diet of only the highest-quality ingredients in a balance that keeps fat to a minimum (keep nuts and seeds to a minimum) and that includes about 15 to 20 percent protein. This should be supplemented by

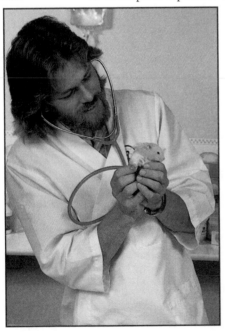

fresh clean water served in a clean water bottle with a functional sipping tube.

Your pet's housing, whether it be a glass or plastic aquarium or a wire cage, should be kept clean. Soiled bedding should be removed daily and bedding changed completely every week. A clean, dry enclosure positioned in a spot out of drafts or direct sunlight is one of the most effective tools in the keeping of a healthy hamster—and in the rehabilitation of an ailing one.

Your hamster's stress levels should also be kept at a minimum, as stress is one of the primary contributors to the deterioration of hamster health. While stress itself is not a

disease-carrying agent, its presence in a hamster's life opens
the door to bacteria and viruses that can harm the animal's
organs and immune system. Keep stress under control by
adhering to a routine in the hamster's care and to the maintenance and cleanliness of his habitat, and by restricting his
interactions only to those individuals who respect the hamster and understand how to handle him correctly. Housing
each hamster alone in his own roomy abode is also important in keeping stress low and preserving hamster health.

Quarantines

It is wise when bringing a new hamster into the household
to quarantine him for a few weeks to ensure he doesn't bring
in contagious illnesses that might infect existing pet hamsters. While the newcomer should be offered his own habitat, that habitat should be kept in a separate room during
those first weeks. While it goes without saying that a new
hamster, for his own safety as well as that of the other pets,
should never be brought home and simply placed into an
existing pet's habitat, some illnesses can be airborne, so
a more formalized quarantine is necessary to ensure that
all of the hamsters are healthy and present no danger to
each other.

Changes with Aging

Even the most diligent adherence to preventive measures can
not grant a pet hamster immortality. After his first or second
birthday, you will begin to notice some changes that are
common to a hamster as he ages. There may be some hair
loss, some diminishment of energy levels and some subtle
changes in the daily routine. The observant owner, however,
will know when a change, even a minimal one, calls for
medical attention.

Diseases and Conditions
Allergies

Some hamsters may have allergies to certain foods and types
of bedding. You may notice that your hamster is sneezing

and his eyes are runny but his behavior has not changed. He may have red feet and have dry, flaky skin with some hair loss. These symptoms point to allergies, which can be treated in various ways. First, your hamster may be allergic to his food. Try feeding him a simple diet with a reduction of protein. Easily digestible foods such as white rice or white bread, fruit and vegetables and cereal (like corn flakes) are favorable. Next, try changing your hamster's bedding; he may be allergic to the filler (such as sawdust). Other causes of allergies are strong odors such as cleaning agents, cologne and cigarette smoke. Once you determine what your pet is allergic to, removal of the irritant should provide relief.

Colds

Just like humans, hamsters are susceptible to colds and can actually catch a cold from you! A good preventative measure is to keep your hamster away from drafts and severe drops in temperature. Hamsters should be kept at a moderate room temperature.

> **Classic Signs of Wet Tail**
>
> - watery diarrhea and, consequently, moisture around the hamster's tail
> - loss of appetite
> - dehydration
> - unkempt hair
> - rectal bleeding or rectal prolapse
> - uncharacteristic irritability
>
> A wet tail can also indicate a bladder or uterine infection or a number of other serious illnesses in hamsters. No matter what the cause, wet tail is a symptom that should be evaluated by a veterinarian immediately—the sooner the better.

If your hamster has symptoms such as a runny nose, watery eyes, sneezing and lethargy, he most likely has the sniffles. He will probably be curled up in a corner and may feel cool to the touch. A cold in a hamster can quickly turn into life threatening pneumonia. Therefore he must be treated immediately by first putting his cage in a warm area that is free from drafts. An artificial light source can be put near the cage and bedding material should be abundant to provide your hamster with additional warmth. A luke-warm solution of equal parts milk and water with a teaspoon of honey should be given to your hamster. Take your hamster to the veterinarian after two days if you don't see improvement.

Constipation

Symptoms of constipation in a hamster are a distended (enlarged) belly, lethargy and arching of the back. He most likely will not want to be held or petted because of the discomfort. Lack of exercise and a decrease of wet fruit or vegetables can cause constipation. Your hamster may be so uncomfortable that he does not want to eat at all. In that case, you can use an eye dropper to give him a few drops of medicinal paraffin or olive oil. The oil is usually very effective in clearing up the constipation. As your hamster is feeling better, give him plenty of wet greens (such as lettuce).

Diarrhea

Feeding your hamster green vegetables is important, but you don't want to overfeed him or suddenly change his diet. If this happens, you will notice a very messy cage and a dirty hamster due to his loose droppings. Giving him only dry food will usually help him recover quickly. If the problem is severe, a few drops of charcoal (dissolved in water) should do the trick. You should slowly introduce green foods into the diet again, but in moderate amounts.

Heatstroke

Your hamster's cage should not be kept in direct sunlight or too close to a heat source because it is very easy for him to overheat. Clean, easily accessible drinking water should be available to your hamster at all times. If his fur is damp, he seems unresponsive and you can't get a wakeful reaction, speedy action must be taken. You should begin cooling your hamster by pouring cold water over him and making him drink. If he doesn't seem completely back to himself shortly, you should take him to the veterinarian right away.

Wet Tail

Perhaps the most prevalent disease in the pet hamster population is the condition known commonly as wet tail, scientifically as *proliferative ileitis*. This is a bacterial illness that causes severe diarrhea in a hamster that can, and often does, prove fatal.

All too common among newly acquired hamsters, wet tail is caused by a bacteria, but that bacteria's ability to gain a foothold in the animal's system is directly linked to conditions within the animal's environment that make his system friendly to bacterial infection.

Stress, for example, is considered an important factor in the proliferation of wet tail (and explains why the disease is so prevalent in young hamsters during their early days in new homes), as are sudden changes in diet, habitat overcrowding, extreme temperatures and unsanitary living conditions.

Although wet tail is most common in young weanling hamsters, it may affect older hamsters as well, so owners should remain attuned to the symptoms—especially when new hamsters join the household. Wet tail is most often discovered in a household with new pets, the hamsters having contracted the disease at the pet shop or breeding facility from which they came. Owners are advised to watch for the telltale signs of the disease during the first few weeks of a new hamster's presence in his new home. Keeping any newcomers quarantined during those first few weeks is critical due to the highly contagious nature of this condition.

Pocket Pets Need Veterinary Care

From their own surveys on pet owners and veterinary care, the American Veterinary Medical Association has found that only about 5.02 percent of hamster owners seek veterinary care for their pets, and that's a shame. All pets, from the tiniest mouse or frog to the most expensive champion show dog, should receive necessary veterinary attention.

Hamsters have a relatively short life span, yet when we become owners we commit to all aspects of their care, including their medical care. In keeping with this philosophy, there are more veterinarians today who are experienced in caring for small and exotic animals, and more opportunities for hamster owners to seek help when their hamsters need it. Some practitioners even offer discounts to people who come to them with small animals in need of treatment.

The ultimate goal is to educate the public at large that hamsters are just as worthy of medical care as any member of the family, whether they be two-legged or four. It is acceptable, necessary and part of that grand commitment that is pet ownership.

TREATMENT

Treatment usually involves the administration of a combination of anti-biotics, fluid therapy and anti-diarrhea medications. Since medicating a hamster is a delicate task, only the veterinarian should direct such treatment. Hamsters, for example, can have severe reactions to antibiotics as well as over-the-counter remedies that promise results. It's essential that you pursue veterinary treatment at the earliest sign of a problem.

Aside from following the veterinarian's treatment regimen, keep the sick hamster away from any healthy ones in the household, and keep his habitat clean, warm and dry. A hamster's survival of wet tail is directly linked to the quality of nursing the hamster receives from his owners, and to the quality of his environment.

Preventive Antibiotics?

One controversial practice being promoted recently is the prevention of wet tail through the routine administration of antibiotics to a new hamster, whether or not he exhibits any signs of disease, just as you would vaccinate a new puppy. But because antibiotics present their own threat to hamsters, routine treatment of healthy hamsters may not only be dangerous, but also bring about an unexpected side effect. Over-treating the hamster with antibiotics without due cause and veterinary supervision may cause drug resistance. This will cause the antibiotics to be ineffective to the hamster should he require antibiotic therapy in the future for an actual illness.

Hair and Skin Problems

Hair Loss As your hamster ages, natural changes will occur in his skin and hair—a thinning or loss of hair, a thickening or blemishing of the skin, etc. Upon close examination of the hamster's daily activities, you may find that hair loss is being caused by the animal's rubbing up against rough surfaces within his enclosure. It's important to note that skin and hair changes should be closely monitored because they can indicate more serious health concerns.

If, for example, hair loss is accompanied by a hamster's increased thirst, you are looking at the classic signs of adrenal disease, the treatment for which includes the surgical removal of the adrenal gland(s). Other possibilities for the cause of these symptoms include thyroid disease or, in females, disease of the reproductive tract.

Parasites   Hair loss and skin problems can also be caused by parasites, the most common parasites affecting hamsters

being demodex mites, which cause demodectic mange. What's interesting about this condition is that mites are common and typically benign residents on hamsters, yet they can become a problem if the host hamster develops a more serious internal illness. That illness opens the door to a severe mite infestation, the successful treatment for which is curing the illness (then the mites). Like all serious conditions that afflict hamsters, this, too, should be presented to the veterinarian for treatment.

Abscesses   Hamsters are also prone to abscesses, so the owner should also be on the

Always get a veterinarian's advice before administering first aid to an injured hamster.

lookout for lumps and bumps on the skin. The most common causes of these skin anomalies are abscesses and tumors. While abscesses, which can be quite painful if ignored, will on occasion open and drain on their own; in most cases this must be done by the veterinarian. Tumors, too, may require surgical removal depending on their type and where they are located on the hamster's body.

Scratching   Hamsters are meticulously clean, but incessant, compulsive scratching is not part of the normal grooming program. The hamster driven to this may be suffering from a parasite infestation, adrenal disease, a fungal infection, liver disease, a dietary imbalance or a lack of particular nutrients. Allergies to either food or elements in the environment (such as dusty or aromatic bedding, chemical disinfectants or shampoos) can also cause abnormal scratching behavior.

Injuries

Bleeding   Bleeding can be a sign of cancer, problems with digestive organs or a prolapsed rectum (bleeding from the rectum is especially serious in that it can indicate tumors, cancer, ulcers or intestinal problems), as well as an external injury to the hamster. This can be something as minor as a superficial cut on a leg from an exposed wire in the cage, to a foot injury from an overzealous run on the wheel, or something as severe as a bite wound from a fellow hamster that objects to sharing a habitat.

If your hamster is experiencing hair loss, start by checking the cage for rough surfaces that may be causing irritation.

Treatment   Any type of bleeding should warrant an immediate call to the veterinarian for advice on how the hamster's particular case should be handled. He may require on-site veterinary attention to stop the bleeding or simple nursing care at home. The doctor may suggest that you administer hydrogen peroxide or betadine on a cotton swab to keep the wound clean and free of infection.

Follow the veterinarian's advice on how to deal with the wound, even with treatment as seemingly simple as the choice and application of topical antibiotic ointments or similar medications. Great care must be taken as some preparations can be absorbed into the hamster's system through the skin, and prove to be toxic or even fatal. This problem may be exacerbated if the hamster licks at the wound, thus taking even more of the substance into his system.

Respiratory Problems

Infections The primary cause of breathing problems can be directly related to the respiratory system. A viral or bacterial infection, for example, may be the root of the problem. A viral infection relies on a hamster's healthy immune system to facilitate recovery; a bacterial infection may require antibiotic therapy under the direction of a veterinarian.

Some hamsters experience respiratory problems due to bedding dust.

Environmental Causes Components within the hamster's environment may also be to blame for the animal's breathing difficulties, such as dusty or aromatic bedding materials (which can also harm the animal's liver), cold drafts that infiltrate the hamster's habitat or allergens or chemical fumes in the hamster's atmosphere.

Underlying Problems Difficulty breathing may signal a more severe internal illness, such as a heart problem, that breaks down the respiratory system. Respiratory problems caused by an underlying, and typically even more serious, health condition can be corrected only by addressing that primary condition first. The veterinarian must be contacted immediately at the onset of respiratory symptoms, as this is the person best equipped to determine what is the root of respiratory distress in your hamster.

Unexpected Pregnancy

As we have seen, there is no shortage of hamsters on the pet market. Unfortunately, good permanent homes for the many hamsters bred and born each year are not abundant. In light of this situation, intentionally breeding your hamster, unless you intend to keep all of the offspring you produce for the duration of their lives, is not a particularly responsible avenue to pursue.

Some people believe they can make money from breeding hamsters. Another motivation for breeding among pet owners is the assumption that this is the ideal way to teach the kids "the miracle of life." Again, these ideas fail to take into account the well-being of the hamsters and the often insurmountable challenge of finding good, permanent homes for them—thus imparting an additional, much sadder, lesson to the children about pet overpopulation and homelessness. When entertaining the idea of breeding, pet owners are wise to remind themselves that they bought this animal for companionship. They brought him into their home for the opportunity to coexist with a species so different from their own, to revel in how blessed we humans are to be able to adopt such creatures and

Daily interaction with your hamster will help you evaluate any health changes.

live happily in their presence. In most cases, breeding is best kept out of the equation.

Unfortunately, sometimes accidents happen. With hamsters this often occurs at the beginning of the owner/hamster relationship with an owner who has no intention of breeding his or her pets. This individual discovers several weeks after bringing a pair of allegedly female hamsters home, that those two hamsters have become a family of seven, eight, maybe nine. Such owners will need a crash course in the care of that new little family, both to help them survive, and to prevent a repeat performance in the future.

A litter of six baby hamsters.

Breeding Basics

Hamsters boast one of the quickest reproduction rates in the animal kingdom. Reaching sexual maturity at about two months of age, hamster gestation is also phenomenally short—about sixteen days. No wonder the hamster isn't anywhere near the threat of extinction.

When kept in captivity as pets, hamsters are sometimes housed together, but instinctively they prefer a solitary existence. The classic wild hamster, however, would typically come together with other hamsters only for breeding, after which they would go their separate ways, leaving the female to raise her young as a single mother.

Hamster breeders today tend to follow this same natural pattern: housing the hamsters separately, placing a female in estrus with the designated male only at the opportune time. Even then, the caretaker must watch the pair carefully. A female who doesn't happen to be in the mood can be dangerous to the amorous male in her midst. Therefore, if she isn't ready, it's best to keep the two apart until she is (and to remove the male after a successful mating has taken place).

About two weeks later, the female will be ready to give birth. Before this occurs, the owner should clean her enclosure and replace the bedding with a thick layer of clean shavings, for she will have to remain undisturbed with her young for the first couple of weeks after they are born.

It's best not to interfere while the hamster prepares a nest for her litter.

As her due date approaches, the mother-to-be will become restless. This is the signal that her owner should refrain from handling and playing with her. A day or two later, as if by magic, the owner will probably just happen to notice that suddenly the enclosure is occupied by the new mom and a litter of five to ten naked babies.

Care of the Litter

Hamster mothers don't appreciate interference from humans, so the little family is best left alone for a week or two to prevent stress. If the mother feels stressed or threatened during those first couple of weeks, she may destroy her young. It is best to resist the temptation to get involved and let nature take its course.

As the weeks pass, the young hamsters will sprout hair, begin to share their mother's solid food (although they will not be completely weaned until they are almost a month old) and begin to venture farther away from mom's side. Before you know it, they too will look at the world with that cheeky, whimsical expression that sets the hamster apart from all other rodents and has made the hamster famous.

The owner of these hamsters is then faced with the challenge of placing the young animals into new and permanent homes. While siblings can usually coexist for a while, you may have to separate them if placing them takes longer than you intended. And indeed that is the hard part. The breeding is easy, the responsibility of placement is tough, and not something the unsuspecting new owner—the accidental breeder—ever expects to have to deal with.

When faced with this responsibility, your best option is to contact the local animal shelter(s). Whether or not they are adopting hamsters themselves, you can ask them to refer people looking for hamster pets to you. You will need to screen potential owners who are interested in adopting. You should ask about their families, other pets, living situation, hamster knowledge etc. Gauge their commitment to this little pet and be sure they are serious about the responsibility.

Remember that releasing pet animals into the wild is not only cruel, it also wreaks havoc with native wildlife by interfering with their food chain and natural habitat. If you come to the point where you simply cannot find proper homes for the hamsters or keep them yourself, euthanasia may be the only alternative, performed either at the animal shelter or by your own veterinarian.

This is unfortunate but far more humane and responsible than seeing hamsters go to inappropriate homes, or releasing them into the wild to face starvation, injury, illness and countless other dangers for which they are not prepared. When all is said and done, share your experiences with other new owners. Education about the pitfalls of breeding will do them and their pets a favor, as well as the hamster species as a whole.

part three
Enjoying Your

Understanding
Your
Hamster

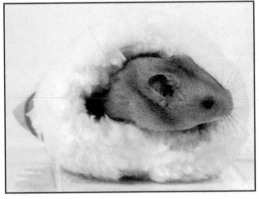

Imagine that you are just 5 inches long, stand only 2 inches tall and weigh only a few ounces.

Imagine, too, that your natural instincts tell you, the diminutive critter that you are, that you should sleep by day safely hidden in solitude within tunnels beneath the ground, and awaken in the evening to hunt for food under the cover of darkness.

Yet despite these powerful callings, you find yourself in a household of odd two-legged creatures who tower above you; who hoist you into the air, away from the safety of your beloved terra firma, often waking you from your peaceful day's slumber to do so. Even though you prefer living alone, you may have to coexist with another hamster and share your enclosure as well as your food.

A Hamster's Perspective

Think about it. This is how we must look to the hamsters in our lives—and how they must perceive humans. Viewed in this light, our world must be a pretty scary place for these tiny animals.

But our world need not, nor should it be, a frightening place for the hamster. In the right caretaker's hands, hamsters can be amazingly adaptable little creatures. We can use this characteristic to our mutual benefit: to make life more pleasant for the hamster and to make her care as simple as possible for us.

The first step in this noble mission is to take the time to learn all that you can about this unique little creature, and then to make the effort to see our world through her eyes. Through this fascinating, educational journey, you will learn that the hamster is more than willing to work with her owners in forging the unique bond that can result in a mutually satisfying relationship between owner and pocket pet.

In getting to know the hamster, you will also learn—we would hope not by experience, of course—that stress can take a profound physical and emotional toll on this tiny animal. Seeing the world through your hamster's eyes is the first step toward preventing stress in your pet's life. The hamster who comes into the care of an individual who has made this effort is a lucky hamster indeed.

A compassionate owner is able to look at the world from the hamster's perspective.

Will the Real Hamster Please Stand Up?

Most people you meet assume they understand hamsters. What's to understand? They are quiet little rodents without a care in the world who eat, sleep and sometimes run on a wheel. There's not much more to them, is there? If you look at the misconceptions that people have about hamsters, you may be surprised by what you'll learn about the true hamster personality.

Misconception   Hamsters are easy-care pets and don't require much interaction with their owners.

Fact   Hamsters do require attention from their owners. They thrive on it. And this must be provided on a regular routine basis, not just when the owner removes the hamster from her cage once a week for her routine cleaning. Though hamsters are not crazy about others of their own kind, they, for some reason, tend to enjoy the company of humans. This bond, however, takes time to develop and is not something that can be forced from your hamster.

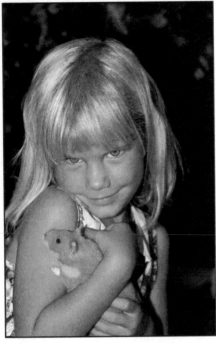

Misconception   Hamsters are annoying, all they do is run endlessly on their wheels all night, keeping everyone awake with the wheel's squeaking.

Fact   Those who know and work with hamsters, whether they be pet owners, veterinarians or animal welfare activists, know that far too many hamsters are lonely hamsters left in

Your hamster will thrive on lots of consistent love and affection from you—the more the better.

their cages with little or nothing to do. Hamsters can't bark like dogs to alert their owners to their loneliness. They don't chew up shoes or destroy furniture in blatant exhibitions of frustration. They have no choice but to languish within their cages, sleeping even more than they would like to, perhaps eating more than they need to and running endlessly on a squeaky wheel that is their only outlet for exercise.

The hamster would prefer to eat, sleep, burrow into the bedding of their enclosure, play with a variety of toys and, yes, spend a bit of time each day interacting with her owners.

Misconception Hamsters are nasty, difficult to socialize and are prone to biting.

Fact Depending on your pet's personality, with proper, gradual and gentle handling, she may choose to trust and respond to you and perhaps one or two other people, or she may take a more openly social approach and embrace all humans who enter her realm. Either way, respect the animal for what she is most comfortable with. The hamster in turn will respect you and reward you with her own brand of hamster affection. Socialize your hamster gently and gradually to a variety of people and experiences at an early age. Establish a set routine for your pet, allow her to nap peacefully and undisturbed during the day, protect her from rough handling, loud voices and sounds and household dangers.

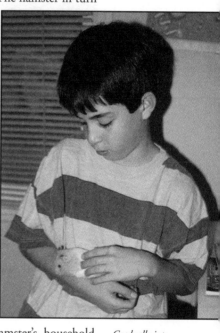

Gradually introducing your hamster to new people when she is young will result in a more trusting pet.

Hamsters and Other Pets

While socialization, especially at a young age, is an important element to the upbringing of the healthy, well-adjusted hamster, this is best limited only to the humans in the hamster's household and their human friends and relatives. While we may enjoy envisioning that all pets coexist and interact happily with one another, from the dog and cat all the way to the tiny hamster, fostering such a scene with the hamster is not a good idea.

Yes, you may have seen a photograph of a large dog resting peacefully alongside an inquisitive hamster. But such a scene will only stress the hamster—a tiny prey animal, after all—that is forced to interface unprotected with a large predator. An animal lover who shares his or her home with a variety of species is wise to respect each of those animals: not to tease the cat by dangling a delectable hamster in its face, or to stress that hamster by presenting her to the resident predator. The hamster will live just as happily—and probably longer—if she never interacts with other family pets. The only family member she needs is you.

The Escape Artist

Hamsters are consummate escape artists. Far too many hamster owners learn this the hard way. When owners compare hamster stories, you're likely to hear fantastic tales of hamster escapes and, hopefully, lost hamster recoveries. Understand this animal's propensity to run, take it seriously, and you can prevent your hamster from getting lost.

The escapes usually occur because of human error. The cage door is left open; the hamster is allowed to run unsupervised through the house; the hamster is housed in a wooden enclosure that proves no match to the animal's gnawing abilities; or perhaps a child is left to care for the animal when he or she is either too young for such a responsibility or uninterested in expending the necessary energy.

Hamster Hideouts

Did you turn your back for a moment and your pet made a run for it? Look in dark spots; check your stacks of magazines and newspapers; check inside sofa cushions, mattresses, and boxes of any sort. Listen for scuffling or scratching sounds nearby. Hamsters love to burrow, so chances are she is dozing in a cozy self-made nest.

Sometimes the hamster takes advantage of a situation and creates her own escape route—and writes her own story. She the dog cleans. Excessive, darker discharge with a foul odor is indicative of infection. Your veterinarian will show you how to treat it.

The Female (Bitch)

Mammary gland tumors—half of which are malignant in female dogs—are virtually eliminated by having the bitch spayed prior to the onset of sexual maturity (or the first estrus), which normally occurs at about six months of age. The same is true of cancer of the uterus.

Pyometra is another very serious disease in which the uterus fills with pus. It is fatal if not promptly treated. But it is entirely preventable: Have your bitch spayed.

Vaginitis can be detected by excessive licking of the vulva in the bitch's effort to clean herself. The hair around the vulva may be stained. Another sign is painful urination. The infection is treated with antibiotics and douches.

Spaying is discussed on page 64.

First Aid and Emergencies

Your puppy cannot tell you when he is sick, but if you spend enough time with him and are observant of his behavior, you'll notice when he's feeling off.

First aid is what you do to assist a dog in an emergency situation before you reach the vet's office. Such assistance should be minimal, so as not to make matters worse, and it must be safe for the dog and its rescuer. If possible, alert the veterinarian immediately.

The first rule of canine first aid is for the rescuer to remain completely calm and (outwardly at least) in control of the situation. The second rule is to fight off the desire to pick up or lean over to comfort a hurt dog face-to-face the way you would a child. When hurt and frightened, a dog's instinct for self-preservation takes over; it is likely to bite whatever comes near. That's where safety comes in.

In an Emergency

If something happens to your puppy during non-regular veterinary visiting hours, it's important to have an emergency number to call. Ask your veterinarian for this number on your first visit and keep it by the phone. You won't want to be scrambling for it when a real emergency strikes. And you won't want to be struggling with directions in the middle of the night if you've never been to the emergency clinic before. It's a good idea to do a practice run to the emergency clinic during a non-emergency. You'll need all the calm you can muster in a real emergency, and knowing how long it will take to get to the clinic is important.

Typical First-Aid Situations

When you notice anything unusual in the way your puppy is acting, ask yourself these questions:

> What caused you to think there was a problem?
>
> What was your first clue there was something wrong?
>
> Is your puppy eating normally?
>
> Does your puppy have a temperature? (Instructions on how to take your puppy's temperature are on page 63.)
>
> What do his stools look like?
>
> Is your puppy limping?
>
> When you do a hands-on exam, is he sore anywhere? Can you feel a lump? Is anything red or swollen?
>
> Write down anything you've noticed. When you call your veterinarian, be prepared to give specific details.

Restraints   Having established the fact that hurting dogs bite, before attempting to muzzle him, be certain he is breathing normally since limited breathing could be made worse by keeping the dog's mouth closed. Don't have a muzzle handy? No problem. A neck-tie, pantyhose, two feet of rope or a dog leash will do nicely. Tie a loose knot in the middle and slip the loop of the knot over the middle of the dog's nose. Pull it firm and tie the two ends under the dog's chin, then in back of the dog's ears. (Make that last tie a bow so it will untie easily to pull forward and off the nose.)

Dogs with short noses or no discernible bridge, such as Pugs, Pekingese and Bulldogs, are not candidates for a makeshift muzzle. In fact, don't do anything that might interfere with their breathing. If you have assistance, a rolled-up blanket, towel or a pillow can be held (gently, but firmly) around the dog's neck while treating the injury.

Shock   Many things such as dehydration or poisoning cause a dog to go into shock, but being hit by a car is the major cause of shock. Since "shock" refers to the breakdown of the cardiovascular system, immediate veterinary care is essential.

Electrical shock   is the fate of a puppy left to chew on an electric cord his owner forgot to put up out of reach. The result is a nasty burn to the mouth which, while painful, will heal in time. More serious are lightning strikes or touching downed wires, as in either case the dog (if not killed) is burned and also suffers circulatory (heart) collapse and pulmonary (lung) edema. If the dog is unconscious and not breathing, give artificial respiration. No matter what the condition, get to a veterinarian immediately.

Hit by car   Automobiles still account for most canine deaths, which is a sad commentary on our responsible dog ownership. All it takes to keep your dog safe is a leash or a fence and basic obedience training. No matter how slight the injury may seem, any dog hit by a car requires immediate

---

A First-Aid Kit

Keep a canine first-aid kit on hand for general care and emergencies. Check it periodically to make sure liquids haven't spilled or dried up, and replace medications and materials after they're used. Your kit should include:

Activated charcoal tablets

Adhesive tape (1 and 2 inches wide)

Antibacterial ointment (for skin and eyes)

Aspirin (buffered or enteric-coated, not Ibuprofen)

Bandages: Gauze rolls (1 and 2 inches wide) and dressing pads

Cotton balls

Diarrhea medicine

Dosing syringe

Hydrogen peroxide (3%)

Petroleum jelly

Rectal thermometer

Rubber gloves

Rubbing alcohol

Scissors

Tourniquet

Towel

Tweezers

emergency treatment by a veterinarian. There may be internal injuries or bleeding, broken bones, concussion and so forth. (See "Shock," above.)

Check for external bleeding and stop it by applying a pressure bandage or just holding a bandage or clean padded cloth over the wound. Spurting blood indicates a severed artery, which can also be controlled by applying pressure on the artery.

Moving an injured dog other than a very small one requires two people and a board (bench, sled or any improvised stretcher) or a blanket held taut. Do not muzzle a dog in shock, but keep the dog quiet and transfer him immediately to the veterinarian's.

When a board is the means of transportation, be sure the dog is securely tied to it with strips of sheeting or rope. An injured animal panics easily and could do itself further damage in struggling to escape.

Life-Saving Procedures

There are three things you should know how to do that could instantly save your dog's life. Artificial respiration, to start the dog breathing again, and heart massage, used when no heartbeat can be felt or heard, together form the well-known **CPR** (for cardio-pulmonary resuscitation). The **Heimlich maneuver** is the method used to dislodge a foreign object that is causing the dog to choke.

Chest Compression

The easiest way to administer artificial respiration is by compressing the chest. Here is the five-step method for chest compression:

1. Feel or listen for a pulse or heartbeat.

2. Clear the mouth of secretions and foreign objects. (You might have to use the Heimlich maneuver to remove an obstruction that's out of reach.)

3. Lay the dog on his *right* side on a flat surface.

4. Place both hands on the chest and press down sharply, releasing immediately.

   (If you do *not* hear air going in and out, switch to the mouth-to-nose method.)

5. Continue until the dog is breathing on his own, or as long as the heart is beating.

Mouth-to-Nose Method   Follow steps 1 and 2 above, then

3. Pull the tongue forward and keep the lips closed with your hand.

4. Take a breath and, with your mouth over the dog's nose, blow a steady stream of air for three seconds.

5. Release to let the air out. Continue until the dog is breathing or as long as the heart is beating.

Heart Massage

When heart massage is combined with mouth-to-nose resuscitation (it takes two people), it is canine CPR. Heart massage alone, however, also brings air to the lungs.

To perform, follow steps 1 and 2 above for artificial respiration, then for *small dogs and puppies:*

3. Standing in back of the dog, place one hand on the sternum (bottom of chest) behind the dog's elbow with your thumb on top, fingers beneath.

4. With the other hand above your thumb, over the heart, press the chest firmly six times. Count to five (to let the chest expand) and repeat until the heart is beating or no heartbeat is felt for five minutes.

For *large dogs,* follow the same procedure but place the heel of your hand on the rib cage behind the elbow (which will be over the heart).

The Heimlich Maneuver

This is the method used to clear the dog's air passage when he's choking. He'll be breathing hard, coughing, pawing at his mouth and in a panic. Put one hand over his nose, pressing down on his lips with your thumb and forefinger. With your other hand, press down the lower jaw to pry his mouth open.

If you can't see anything or feel anything with a finger, lay the dog on his side and lower his head by putting a pillow under his hindquarters. On a puppy or small dog, place one hand a couple of inches below the bottom of his ribcage (the sternum) and the other hand on the dog's back for support. (On a larger dog, place both hands below the sternum.) Press sharply in and up. Keep it up until the foreign object is dislodged. What you are doing is literally "knocking the air out of him" so the object is expelled by the force of the air. Should the dog be unconscious, do artificial respiration and get on your way to the veterinarian.

Burns are caused by many things, such as touching a hot surface, fire and even sunburn. Severe burn of any kind can proceed to shock and the prognosis is poor. Small superficial burns can be treated by soaking with cold water or ice packs for fifteen to twenty minutes just to relieve the pain. Then trim surrounding hair, wash with surgical soap and gently blot dry. Apply antibiotic ointment. If the area needs protection (for example, when the dog lies down or walks), wrap it loosely with gauze.

Bleeding is one of the primary concerns for first aid. Bleeding of a minor wound can be stopped by first cleaning the area with antiseptic and applying a gauze pad, then bandaging with even pressure using gauze or any clean available material. Watch

Identifying Your Dog

It's a terrible thing to think about, but your dog could somehow, someday, get lost or stolen. How would you get him back? Your best bet would be to have some form of identification on your dog. You can choose from a collar and tags, a tattoo, a microchip or a combination of these three.

Every dog should wear a buckle collar with identification tags. They are the quickest and easiest way for a stranger to identify your dog. It's best to inscribe the tags with your name and phone number; you don't need to include your dog's name.

There are two ways to permanently identify your dog. The first is a tattoo, placed on the inside of your dog's thigh. The tattoo should be your social security number or your dog's AKC registration number.

The second is a microchip, a rice-sized pellet that's inserted under the dog's skin at the base of the neck, between the shoulder blades. When a scanner is passed over the dog, it will beep, notifying the person that the dog has a chip. The scanner will then show a code, identifying the dog. Microchips are becoming more and more popular and are certainly the wave of the future.

for signs of swelling or discoloration below the bandage which indicates a loss of circulation, in which case loosen or remove the bandage immediately.

Arterial bleeding comes in bright red spurts and requires a thick pressure pad (as above) plus additional pressure applied by hand. A tourniquet can be applied to the tail or leg above the wound, between the wound and the heart, but it must be loosened every twenty-five to thirty minutes and is best left to a professional.

Poison Control

Because puppies are so curious, they are prone to getting into any number of potentially toxic substances. These include houseplants, outdoor plants, household substances like cleaning products, pesticides and medications, and other chemical-based products like paint thinner, kerosene and so on. One of the most deadly substances is antifreeze, which tastes sweet to dogs. A few licks result in kidney damage. Only slightly more than that ends in death. Get veterinary help at once. There is no home treatment.

Puppies that spend a lot of time outside may encounter rabid wildlife. Be sure your pup is vaccinated against rabies, and if you see wildlife acting strangely, tell an animal control officer. (Brittany)

About Aspirin Aspirin is not toxic to dogs at doses recommended by a veterinarian, though it has been known to cause stomach irritation. It's best to give a dog a buffered or enteric-coated aspirin. Tylenol, ibuprofen and naproxen sodium are all toxic to dogs.

The National Animal Poison Control Center (NAPCC) provides service twenty-four hours a day, with forty-four licensed veterinarians and board-certified toxicologists to aid you. When you call **1-800-548-2423** you will be charged thirty dollars per case (only payable by credit card) and there's no charge for follow-up calls. Calling **1-900-680-0000** will give you five minutes for $20 plus $2.95 for each additional minute (no follow-ups). Put both numbers with your emergency telephone numbers. Put copies in the glove compartment of your car and in your first aid kit. Be prepared to give your name, address and phone number, what your puppy got into—the amount and how long ago—your pup's breed, age, sex and weight and what reaction the pup is experiencing.

As Your Puppy Ages

It may not seem like he'll ever grow up when he's in the prime of puppyhood, but he will. In fact, dogs can, on the average, live up to 14 years. To live that long in good health, however, your puppy will need your help.

As your puppy ages, you'll notice certain changes. The intense teething period will subside, upward growth will slow down and your puppy will start to "fill out," he'll need less food, his energy level will decrease slightly, and you may even notice greying around his muzzle.

Depending on the kind of dog you have, as he hits middle to old age, your dog's vision will dim, his hearing fade and his joints stiffen. Heart and kidney disease are common in older dogs. Reflexes will not be as sharp as they once were, and your dog may be more sensitive to heat and cold. Your dog may also get grouchy, showing less tolerance to younger dogs, children and other things that may not be part of his normal routine.

Arthritis   Arthritis is common in old dogs. The joints get stiff, especially when it's chilly. Your dog may have trouble getting up in the morning. Make sure he has something soft and warm to sleep on not just at night, but all day. Talk to your veterinarian about treatment; there are pain relievers that can help.

Nutrition   As your dog's activity level slows down, he will need to consume less calories and, as his body ages, he will need less protein. However, some old dogs have a problem digesting foods, too, and this may show up in poor stools and a dull coat. Several dog food manufacturers offer premium quality foods for senior dogs; these foods are more easily digested by the old dog.

Exercise   Exercise is still important to your old dog, who needs the stimulation of walking around and seeing and smelling the world. A leisurely walk around the neighborhood might be enough.

When It's Time

There will come a time when you know your dog is suffering more than he needs to, and you will have to decide how to put him out of his pain. Only you can make the decision, but spare your companion the humiliation of incontinence, convulsions or the inability to stand up or move around. Your veterinarian can advise you on the condition of your dog, but don't let him or her make this decision for you.

When you know it's time, call your veterinarian. He or she can give your dog a tranquilizer, then an injection that is an overdose of anesthetic. Your already sleepy dog will quietly stop breathing. Be there with your dog. Let your arms hold your old friend and let your dog hear your voice saying how much you love him as he goes to sleep. There will be no fear, and the last thing your dog will remember is your love.

Grieving

A well-loved dog is an emotional investment of unparalleled returns. Unfortunately, our dogs' lives are entirely too short and we must learn to cope with inevitably losing them. Grief is a natural reaction to the loss of a loved one, whether it is a pet, a spouse, friend or family member. Grief has no set pattern; its intensity and duration are different for each person and for each loss.

Sometimes the best outlet for grief is a good hard cry. For others, talking about their pet is good therapy. It's especially helpful to talk to people who've also lost an old dog and can relate to your loss. You may want to bury your old friend in a special spot where you can go to remember the wonderful times you shared together. You could also ask your veterinarian about having your dog cremated and keeping his or her ashes in a special urn in your home.

part four

Beyond the Basics

Recommended
Reading

Books
About Health Care

Ackerman, Lowell. *Guide to Skin and Haircoat Problems in Dogs.* Loveland, CO: Alpine Publications, 1994.

Alderton, David. *The Dog Care Manual.* Hauppauge, NY: Barron's Educational Series, Inc., 1986.

American Kennel Club. *American Kennel Club Dog Care and Training.* New York: Howell Book House, 1991.

Bamberger, Michelle, DVM. *Help! The Quick Guide to First Aid for Your Dog.* New York: Howell Book House, 1995.

Carlson, Delbert, DVM, and James Giffin, MD. *Dog Owner's Home Veterinary Handbook.* New York: Howell Book House, 1992.

DeBitetto, James, DVM, and Sarah Hodgson. *You & Your Puppy.* New York: Howell Book House, 1995.

Humphries, Jim, DVM. *Dr. Jim's Animal Clinic for Dogs.* New York: Howell Book House, 1994.

McGinnis, Terri. *The Well Dog Book.* New York: Random House, 1991.

Pitcairn, Richard and Susan. *Natural Health for Dogs.* Emmaus, PA: Rodale Press, 1982.

About Training

Ammen, Amy. *Training in No Time.* New York: Howell Book House, 1995.

Benjamin, Carol Lea. *Dog Problems.* New York: Howell Book House, 1989.

————. Dog *Training for Kids.* New York: Howell Book House, 1988.

————. *Mother Knows Best.* New York: Howell Book House, 1985.

————. *Surviving Your Dog's Adolescence.* New York: Howell Book House, 1993.

Dunbar, Ian, PhD, MRCVS. *Dr. Dunbar's Good Little Dog Book,* James & Kenneth Publishers, 2140 Shattuck Ave. #2406, Berkeley, CA 94704. (510) 658–8588. Order from the publisher.

————. *How to Teach a New Dog Old Tricks,* James & Kenneth Publishers. Order from the publisher; address above.

————. and Gwen Bohnenkamp. *Booklets on Preventing Aggression; Housetraining; Chewing; Digging; Barking; Socialization; Fearfulness; and Fighting,* James & Kenneth Publishers. Order from the publisher; address above.

Evans, Job Michael. *People, Pooches and Problems.* New York: Howell Book House, 1991.

McMains, Joel M. *Dog Logic—Companion Obedience.* New York: Howell Book House, 1992.

Volhard, Jack and Melissa Bartlett. *What All Good Dogs Should Know: The Sensible Way to Train.* New York: Howell Book House, 1991.

Recommended
Reading

Haggerty, Captain Arthur J. *How to Get Your Pet Into Show Business.* New York: Howell Book House, 1994.

McLennan, Bardi. *Dogs and Kids, Parenting Tips.* New York: Howell Book House, 1993.

Moran, Patti J. *Pet Sitting for Profit, A Complete Manual for Professional Success.* New York: Howell Book House, 1992.

Scalisi, Danny and Libby Moses. *When Rover Just Won't Do, Over 2,000 Suggestions for Naming Your Dog.* New York: Howell Book House, 1993.

Sife, Wallace, PhD. *The Loss of a Pet.* New York: Howell Book House, 1993.

Wrede, Barbara J. *Civilizing Your Puppy.* Hauppauge, NY: Barron's Educational Series, 1992.

Magazines

The AKC GAZETTE, The Official Journal for the Sport of Purebred Dogs. American Kennel Club, 51 Madison Ave., New York, NY.

Bloodlines Journal. United Kennel Club, 100 E. Kilgore Rd., Kalamazoo, MI.

Dog Fancy. Fancy Publications, 3 Burroughs, Irvine, CA 92718

Dog World. Maclean Hunter Publishing Corp., 29 N. Wacker Dr., Chicago, IL 60606.

Videos

"SIRIUS Puppy Training," by Ian Dunbar, PhD, MRCVS. James & Kenneth Publishers, 2140 Shattuck Ave. #2406, Berkeley, CA 94704. Order from the publisher.

"Training the Companion Dog," from Dr. Dunbar's British TV Series, James & Kenneth Publishers. (See address above.)

The American Kennel Club produces videos on every breed of dog, as well as on hunting tests, field trials and other areas of interest to purebred dog owners. For more information, write to AKC/Video Fulfillment, 5580 Centerview Dr., Suite 200, Raleigh, NC 27606.

Resources

Breed Clubs

Every breed recognized by the American Kennel Club has a national (parent) club. National clubs are a great source of information on your breed. You can get the name of the secretary of the club by contacting:

The American Kennel Club
51 Madison Avenue
New York, NY 10010
(212) 696-8200

There are also numerous all-breed, individual breed, obedience, hunting and other special-interest dog clubs across the country. The American Kennel Club can provide you with a geographical list of clubs to find ones in your area. Contact them at the above address.

Registry Organizations

Registry organizations register purebred dogs. The American Kennel Club is the oldest and largest in this country, and currently recognizes over 130 breeds. The United Kennel Club registers some breeds the AKC doesn't (including the American Pit Bull Terrier and the Miniature Fox Terrier) as well as many of the same breeds. The others included here are for your reference; the AKC can provide you with a list of foreign registries.

American Kennel Club
51 Madison Ave.
New York, NY 10010

United Kennel Club (UKC)
100 E. Kilgore Rd.
Kalamazoo, MI 49001-5598

American Dog Breeders Assn.
P.O. Box 1771
Salt Lake City, UT 84110
(Registers American Pit Bull Terriers)

Canadian Kennel Club
89 Skyway Ave.
Etobicoke, Ontario
Canada M9W 6R4

National Stock Dog Registry
P.O. Box 402
Butler, IN 46721
(Registers working stock dogs)

Orthopedic Foundation for Animals (OFA)
2300 E. Nifong Blvd.
Columbia, MO 65201-3856
(Hip registry)